Modelling the USF *Constellation*

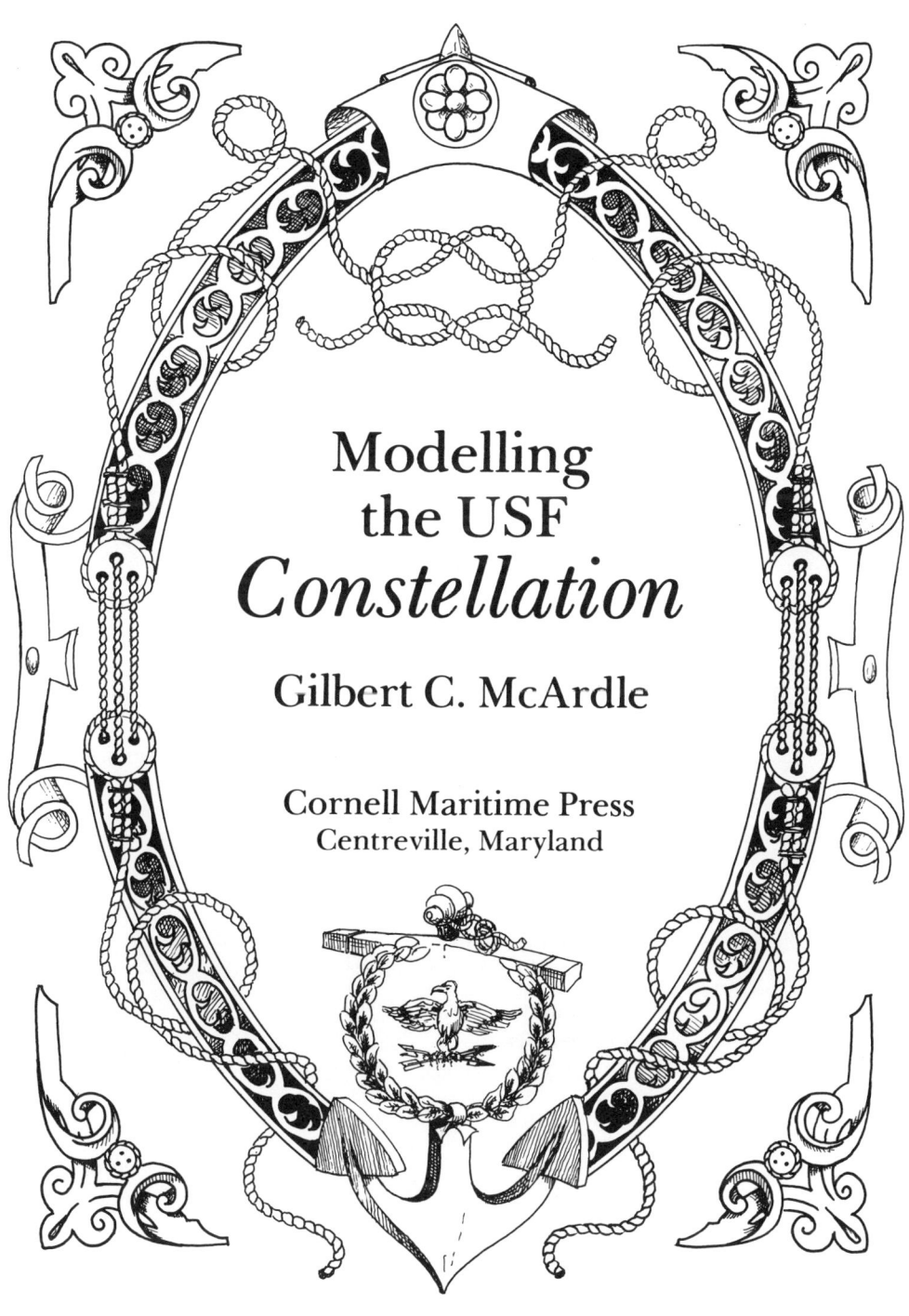

Modelling the USF *Constellation*

Gilbert C. McArdle

Cornell Maritime Press
Centreville, Maryland

To my wife Jackie and our children:
Matthew
Andrew
Daniel
Terrence
Kristin

Copyright © 1985 by Cornell Maritime Press, Inc.

All rights reserved. No part of this book may be used or reproduced in any manner whatsoever without written permission except in the case of brief quotations embodied in critical articles and reviews. For information, address Cornell Maritime Press, Inc., Centreville, Maryland 21617.

    Library of Congress Cataloging-in-Publication Data

McArdle, Gilbert C., 1936-
    Modelling the USF Constellation.

    Bibliography: p.
    Includes index.
    1. Warships—Models.   2. Constellation (Frigate)
I. Title.
VM298.M383   1985   623.8'2015   84-46108
ISBN 0-87033-334-8

Manufactured in the United States of America
First edition, 1985; second printing, 1991

Contents

	List of Illustrations	*vi*
	Preface	*vii*
	Historical Notes on the USF *Constellation*	*x*

PART I HULL

Chapter I	Keel, Stern, Stem, and Rudder	3
Chapter II	Decks and Planking	19

PART II FITTINGS

Chapter III	Stern Section, Quarter Galleries, and Forward Timberheads	44

PART III SPARS AND RIGGING

Chapter IV	Masts and Spars	86
Chapter V	Standing Rigging	108
Chapter VI	Running Rigging	125

	Bibliography	140
	Index	141

List of Illustrations

PHOTOGRAPHS OF THE MODEL

The completed model	*page*	138
Bow detail		138
Stern detail		139
Midship detail		139

PLATES

I.	Gun Deck; Inboard Profile	*facing page*	16
II.	Frames & Half Breadths; Sheer & Body Plan		17
III.	Belaying Pin & Eyebolt Schema; Spar Deck		96
IV.	Rigging Plan		97

Preface

During my first "trip East" when I was ten years old, my father purchased for me *The Built-Up Ship Model,* by Charles E. Davis. Although my father was from coastal Maine, I had been reared in rural Utah and was, therefore, fascinated by Boston and especially in visiting the ship, the USF *Constitution,* and the nautical museums nearby. Although at that age I had some difficulty with the naval nomenclature, Davis's book was clearly written, well illustrated, and served as a major stimulus for me to investigate the particulars of ship modelling. Davis's book was essentially a description of an authentic reproduction of a plank-on-frame construction model of the US Brig *Lexington,* exclusive of spars and rigging. His only departure from the original construction of the brig was in the employment of black walnut trunnelled frames and futtocks which must have been utilized strictly for the rich visual effects obtained from the white wood planking superimposed on dark-colored black walnut frames. (The original *Lexington* had been constructed of white oak frames and planking.) At any rate, the executing of the model was superbly described and served as a basis for my personal lifelong interest in ships and ship models, particularly of full-rigged vessels. Except for a period of study in medical school, when spare time was limited, I found time to complete several ship models and concentrated on plank-on-frame construction which seemed more realistic and challenging as well as giving me more latitude for developing greater detail in construction and modelling. After completing several solid wooden hull model ships, including an approximately three-foot-long model of the USF *Constellation* out of laminated sugar pine, I completed several plank-on-frame construction models from "scratch," including models of the HMS *Victory,* the

Marie Sophie, a merchant brig from a plan of Harold Underhill, and the Baltimore clipper, *Aerial*.

My personal reason for beginning a large scale construction model of the USF *Constellation* stemmed essentially from two events in my life. First of all, I had completed a laminated model of the USF *Constellation* in high school and was, therefore, familiar with some of the general characteristics of the ship. Secondly, and more importantly, during a casual visit in the early 1970s to the site where an active rebuilding of the Inner Harbor in Baltimore, Maryland, was going on, I took my children aboard the *Constellation*, and was immediately impressed with the size and beauty of the ship. I decided then and there to build an authentic reproduction of it. Here it seemed was the ideal opportunity to build a large scale model of an old extant sailing vessel. Because I was in medical practice in Gettysburg, Pennsylvania, which was approximately an hour and a half in time from Baltimore Harbor, I could repeatedly check for details of full-scaled construction whenever necessary. Over the next five to six years, I made periodic trips to the moored *Constellation* and took detailed measurements and drawings including photographs to facilitate each step during the model's construction to clarify details and methods of building.

My initial intention was to attempt to obtain plans from the National Archives or the Baltimore Public Library. However, I soon found that significantly detailed plans from the original draughts were not available. I then thought that by several visits to the *Constellation*, I could measure and make detailed plans of the decks, superstructure, and fitting details from my own measurements. Although visits to the *Constellation* were adequate for sketching and measuring details of deck fittings and rigging, I became aware of the immensity of the project to undertake to measure and record the entire keel and frame structure of the vessel. So, upon the suggestion of my wife, I contacted the naval architect in charge of the renovation project, Mr. Leon Polland. Mr. Polland was immediately cordial and cooperative. He gave me a copy of *The Constellation Question*, (Smithsonian Institution Press, 1970), a spirited history of the controversy that prevailed over the authenticity of the present vessel moored in Baltimore Harbor. (See Historical Notes on the USF *Constellation*.)

I spent approximately seven years of work and research in the construction of the model the *Constellation*. The model was graciously accepted by the members of the *Constellation* Foundation and is presently on display in the World Trade Center of Baltimore's Inner Harbor. This book is essentially a description of the construction of that model and it is hoped that it will serve as a helpful outline for anyone who is interested in making a model of the beautiful *Constellation* presently moored in Baltimore's newly rejuvenated harbor.

In conclusion, I would like to express my thanks to the following individuals: Leon Polland, who kindly provided some of the initial sketched plans of the *Constellation;* to Gordon M. F. Stick, who was helpful in answering my inquiries about donating the model to the *Constellation* Foundation; to the Ethicon Corporation for permission to reproduce a diagram from their *Manual of Operative Procedures;* to Nancy Brennan, who enthusiastically assisted me in transferring and donating the model to the Foundation at the time when she was curator at the *Constellation* dock; to John H. Ensor and Herbert Witz, members of the *Constellation* Foundation, who reviewed the manuscript and encouraged its publication; to Al Weideman, a friend since high school, who offered photographic, technical, and lay out advice; and to Carol Kelley, for her patience in typing from my illegible script.

Historical Notes on the USF *Constellation*

One of the most interesting sagas in the birth and development of the U.S. Navy is the history of the USF *Constellation*. In 1794, the Congress of the United States authorized the construction of six frigates: *United States, Congress, President, Chesapeake, Constitution,* and *Constellation*. When we consider that most of the wooden vessels built as recently as the early portion of the twentieth century have not survived, we can appreciate the near miracle that any wooden vessel of the 1790s has endured to our day. Although rebuilt several times, *Constellation* and *Constitution* are the only wooden vessels even partially intact from that era. The historic *Constellation*, now reconstructed and moored at Baltimore's Inner Harbor, provides an excellent opportunity for the nautical sightseer, educator, historian, researcher, patriot, and especially the modeller to enjoy an educational visit to one of our nation's great historical landmarks. The following, therefore, is an attempt to review the interestingly intricate, and occasionally controversial, history of the USF *Constellation*. For those who plan to construct a model of the *Constellation* and for all others who wish to enhance their appreciation of the fascinating history of this vessel, we offer a brief review.

After Congress authorized construction of the *Constellation*, General Henry Knox, Secretary of George Washington's War Office, engaged the services of Joshua Humphreys, a Philadelphia naval architect. Humphreys then enlisted the services of William Doughty and Josiah Fox, both naval designers, to assist with the making of draughts. It is important to note that all of these frigates had innovative designs, were swift sailers, readily maneuverable, and, although smaller than their equivalent British counterparts, were more than a match for foreign ships of the line. They proved themselves superior time and time again. This is particularly noteworthy because, at the time of their construction, our young nation had only a fledgling and untested navy, not yet respected by maritime powers of the world.

In June of 1794, Thomas Truxtun was appointed captain (the only captain from nonnaval ranks) and superintendent of construction. Naval captains at that time had considerable authority in the construction details and could alter these details if feasible. Truxtun chose David Stodder, on Harris Creek in Baltimore, as the shipwright to construct the vessel. The completed *Constellation* was launched September 7, 1797.

On June 26, 1798, she put to sea, first of the frigates built for the U.S. Navy to be given a military assignment. Her first combat duty was during the quasi-war with France, a war which developed because French privateers and men-of-war were attacking American vessels in the Caribbean. On February 19, 1799, the *Constellation*, under Truxtun, defeated and captured the French 40-gun frigate *L'Insurgente*. One year later, the *Constellation* defeated the much larger 52-gun *La Vengeance*, thus winning a second great naval victory for America.

From 1802 to 1805, the *Constellation* assisted in the blockade of Tripoli in a successful attempt to eliminate piracy against American vessels by the Barbary States of North Africa. During the War of 1812, she prevented a British invasion of Norfolk by defeating the British near the Craney Islands.

An outline of the important dates in the history of the *Constellation* from the War of 1812 to the beginning of the restoration of the vessel in 1958 is as follows:

1815	Assisted in the defeat and capture of the Algerian frigate *Mashuda*.
1819-21	Assisted in protecting Americans off South America.
1825-26	Participated in a sweep against the pirates in the Caribbean Sea.
1829	Was extensively repaired at the Gosport Navy Yard, Norfolk, Virginia, under Chief Naval Architect Lenthall.
1835	Assisted in defeating the Seminoles.
1842	Became the first American warship to visit China.
1843	Helped prevent the British from annexing the Hawaiian Islands.

1845-49   Assisted in carrying food to Ireland during the Great Potato Famine.
1853-55   Was converted to a corvette or sloop of war, at the Gosport Navy Yard, Norfolk, Virginia.
1859-61   Captured three slave ships as flagship of the African squadron.
1861-65   Assisted in protection of Union merchant ships during the Civil War.
1871   Was assigned as a training ship at Annapolis.
1894   Was reassigned as a training ship at Newport, Rhode Island.
1914   Returned to Baltimore for the "Star-Spangled Banner" Centennial Celebration.
1918   Was selected by Assistant Secretary of the Navy, Franklin Delano Roosevelt, to be restored as the oldest ship in the Navy. (The USF *Constitution*, however, was chosen instead.)
1926   Participated in the sesquicentennial celebration of American Independence in Philadelphia.
1940-45   Was appointed by President Franklin Roosevelt auxiliary flagship of the Atlantic Fleet during World War II.
1955   Returned to Baltimore for restoration. Work actually began in 1958.

During the reconstruction-restoration period 1958-1970 extensive historical research was carried out by a special organization, the Baltimore Committee for the Restoration of the *Constellation*. Leon Polland, a naval architect from the Maritime Administration in the United States Department of Commerce, was engaged as Chief of Repair and Reconstruction. Mr. Polland studied the historical record carefully. The result of his investigations was a considerable advance in the state of knowledge of the physical history of the *Constellation* from what it had been in 1918, when Franklin Delano Roosevelt, as Assistant Secretary of the Navy, filed an unsuccessful brief for restoration of the *Constellation* as the oldest ship in the U.S. Navy (instead of the proposed rebuilding of the *Constitution*.)[1] In 1966 Polland made a full report of his findings to the Society of Naval Architects and Marine Engineers.[2] This report provided the necessary guidelines that had been used for reconstruction of the *Constellation*. The proud vessel presently moored in Baltimore's Inner Harbor, and the prototype for the model detailed within this book, reflects in its many features Polland's painstaking search for historical authenticity.

Thus far the story is straightforward and uncomplicated. But reconstructions, whether of ships or any other antique structure, tend to stir up controversies, and the *Constellation* is no exception to this rule. Furthermore, because of the strenuous use to which they are put, wooden vessels are much more subject to the need for repair, maintenance, and rebuilding over the decades and centuries, than, say a dwelling or home. Of the original timbers and fittings of the HMS *Victory*, for example, only ten percent survive in the present reconstruction. The rebuilt *Constitution* probably has an even smaller proportion of its original materials in its present form. The controversy that has arisen concerning the *Constellation* was raised by the noted naval historian Howard Chapelle in 1968.[3] Mr. Chapelle who had made his own study of the historical documents surrounding the building and rebuilding of the *Constellation*, advanced the theory that the original vessel had ceased to exist in 1853. He contended that the vessel was not overhauled at Gosport, but replaced by the construction of an entirely new ship, a corvette, or sloop of war, bearing the same name, *Constellation*. He advanced three main points as confirmatory evidence supporting his opinions as follows:

1) The frame distance (center distance between futtocks) on the original *Constellation* was 26 inches and not 32 inches as on the present reconstructed *Constellation*.
2) The rounded stern and lengthening of the vessel by 12 feet at the time of the reconstruction in 1853 (with use of Lenthall draughts and offsets) was corroborative evidence that the entire ship was rebuilt without utilizing timber from the original *Constellation*.
3) The 1918 Roosevelt memorandum was full of incorrect naval nomenclature and hence contains supportive evidence to show that the present *Constellation* is spurious and does not represent the original vessel.

Mr. Polland's definitive rebuttals to Mr. Chapelle's thesis were thoroughly presented in the book, *The* Constellation *Question,* and the reader-modeller seeking further information about this controversy should consult it.[3] Several of the highlights of the rebuttals to Chapelle's claims, however, deserve brief discussion here.

In regard to his first premise about the distance between the frames of the vessel, Chapelle insisted even years before the publication of his monograph that the distance between the frames of the original *Constellation* was 26 inches as noted on the official draughts of 1794 (Doughty). Since the present *Constellation* had a frame distance of 32 inches, the vessel according to Chapelle, was obviously an imposter. Polland has pointed out several problems with this premise. First of all, no one knows if the "official draught" was ever used for the construction of the *Constellation*. Joshua Humphreys supposedly approved the Doughty draught, but Josiah Fox claimed that his draughts were the ones used for the construction of the *Constellation*. Unfortunately, Fox's draughts do not exist [at the present time]. There is no known extant sail plan by any of the employed naval architects. Commodore Truxtun's communications suggested that he too had a hand in altering the original draught but to what extent no one knows as adequate documentation has not survived. An important item that indicated a weakness in this first of Chapelle's premises was a letter from the shipwright, David Stodder, to the Secretary of the Navy dated April 30, 1795, in which Stodder clearly stated that the frame distance was 32 inches. This obviously disagreed with the "official draught" but *is* the frame distance of the present *Constellation*. Chapelle sloughed off this point by merely stating that in his letter Mr. Stodder "made a mistake"!

The second premise Chapell promulgated was that the present *Constellation* was an entirely new vessel, a sloop of war, or corvette, built at Gosport at the Norfolk Navy Yard in 1853, and verified by the presence of the rounded stern which, according to Chapelle, was not present before 1853. Polland's rebuttal to this argument was fundamentally based on the existence of the Mizzen Mast Survey of 1840, microdated 1829 (in the National Archives, Washington, D.C.) which portrayed the *Constellation* with a rounded stern identical to the present one—obviously long before the 1853 rebuilding. Evan Randolph, a descendant of Commodore Truxtun's, wrote in the *American Neptune*, 1979[4], that there were extensive repairs done on the *Constellation* at Gosport in 1829 as reported by Lenthall, the naval architect in charge of reconstruction, and that the lines and offsets on draughts dated 1853 by Lenthall were in fact taken off by him in 1829. Therefore, the rounded stern probably dates from that time, which would coincide with the date from the Mizzen Mast Survey in the National Archives. This information makes it difficult to accept readily Mr. Chapelle's premise of *Constellation's* complete reconstruction in 1853.

Merritt Edson, editor of the excellent *Nautical Research Journal*, reviewed in a 1978 edition of the *Journal*[5] information gathered by Howard Hoffman (modeller at the Smithsonian Institution) from the log book of the U.S. Navy Yard at Gosport, Virginia, between November 1852 and August 1854 which detailed the reconstruction of the new sloop of war, the *Constellation*. Although no definite conclusions were presented by Mr. Edson, it is implied that this log book verifies the destruction of the "old" *Constellation* and the building of the "new" *Constellation*. In my opinion, the excerpts from the log book do not reflect the *complete* destruction of the vessel, and the much-quoted phrase "hauling out timbers for the *Constellation*" ("hauling out" in this sense means, carrying out timbers from shipyard to vessel) does not clearly define whether these timbers were from the "new" or the "old" *Constellation*. If any portion of the futtocks or frames were salvageable, they would have been used again, or, if not, utilized as templates for the new frames similar to any other ship reconstruction process. Additionally, in the *Nautical Research Journal*, September 1981[6], there are excerpts from the *Statistical History of the Navy of the United States* by Lieut. George F. Emmons, 1850, in which the performance of the *Constellation* in a Mediterranean cruise in 1833 is praised. Furthermore, the *Constellation* helped in preventing the British from annexing the Hawaiian Islands in 1843 (a long sail from Baltimore), and she would have to have been an exceptionally seaworthy vessel at that time to do so.[7]

The third and most tenuous aspect of Mr. Chapelle's thesis concerns his attack on the "inaccurate" naval nomenclature which was used in the Roosevelt "brief" in describing the *Constellation*. For example, terms such as "chain iron" for chainplates, "upper frames" for top-timbers or futtocks, "cut to pieces" for cut in two, "sag at both ends" for hog or hogged, "lowparts" for bottom or underbody, and finally, the use of "cottoned" Chapelle found were impossible to accept as the writing of a competent professional shipbuilder or naval architect. These criticisms of Chapelle's seem picayune. The use of a few amateurish or nonbookish naval terms by a man who did not claim to be an experienced shipwright nor a maritime scholar cannot be construed as direct, negative corroborative evidence for the authenticity of the USF *Constellation*.

In conclusion, what can anyone say about the history of the *Constellation* and its multiple reconstructions? It is obvious that the precise complex methods utilized, and the historical evolution of the changes and alterations of the *Constellation* will probably never be entirely understood unless wood talks or someone resurrects a shipwright from the Baltimore Harris Creek shipyard of the 1790s to tell his story! Uncertainty over the documented changes and educated guesses about the undocumented changes make it clear that the *Constellation* we know is not identical to the one built between 1794 and 1797. Nevertheless, we should be grateful and rejoice in the fact that any form of the *Constellation* exists at the Inner Harbor in Baltimore. The ship does provide a beautiful centerpiece for the harbor and my hope is that it will continue to remain there for people to see and enjoy for many years to come.

Lastly, I do believe that if Commodore Thomas Truxtun could revisit Baltimore for a day or so, he may not agree with all the reconstruction details of the USF *Constellation*, but I know that he would gleefully sail her out of Baltimore Harbor if given the slightest opportunity. Sail ho!

Notes

1. Leon Polland, Charles Scarlett, John Scheid, and Donald Stewart, "Yankee Race Horse: The USS *Constellation*, 1797 to 1979," *Maryland Historical Magazine* 56 (March 1961): 15-31.

2. Leon Polland, "The Frigate *Constellation*: An Outline of Present Restoration," *Society of Naval Architects and Marine Engineers*, (1966): 1-131.

3. Howard I. Chapelle and Leon Polland, *The* Constellation *Question* (Washington, D.C.: Smithsonian Institution Press, 1970).

4. Evan Randolph, "USS *Constellation*, 1797 to 1979," *The American Neptune* (October 1979): 235.

5. *Nautical Research Journal* 24 (November 1978): 151-52.

6. *Nautical Research Journal* 27 (September 1981): 152-53.

7. Leon Polland, et al, "Yankee Race Horse."

Modelling the USF *Constellation*

PART I
HULL

CHAPTER I
Keel, Stern, Stem, and Rudder

Once you have decided to construct a plank-on-frame model of the USF *Constellation* your first step is to decide exactly what size or scale to use. I used a 1/4-in.-to-1-ft scale. This scale afforded adequate size to obtain excellent model detail without being too cumbersome. Also, it is a reasonable scale for a museum type model appropriate for presentation especially when a portion of the deck-and-hull planking are intentionally left off to display many of the inside construction details of a multidecked model. (This particular method for inspection of the "innards" of a ship is similar to the famous English Admiralty models by Samuel Pepys and others in the London Maritime Museum.) A scale of 1/8 in. or 3/32 in. to 1 ft, on the other hand, is a good size for a fireplace mantel model or other methods of home display since the beauty of the plank-on-frame construction can be maintained, and the model is physically less cumbersome to construct and transport.

Base and Support Frame

The baseboard upon which this model was placed during construction was made from a piece of seven ply, 3/4-in. plywood, 1-1/2 ft by 5 ft with 1-in.-by-4-in. edging around the plywood base to prevent warping. These edge boards were mitered and screwed in place with #6, 1-1/2-in. flathead screws, which should be properly countersunk to prevent scratching of the table top or display area. An effort should be made to construct this base as "square" as possible as it will facilitate obtaining measurements which will need to be taken frequently during the construction of the hull. Multiple-scored or pencil-ruled measurements may be made along the front and side edges of the baseboard to additionally facilitate direct model measurements during construction. (It should be noted that although we are in the age of the metric system, the original vessel was built on the English system of feet and inches. Therefore, it is obviously necessary to make the measurements for reduction to scale using this standard system. I recommend using one of those old-time yardstick rulers which were often used as advertisements by furniture stores and affixing it to the periphery of the baseboard with small nails. However, since it is only three feet long, it is eliminated after the early futtock frames are in place as it isn't long enough.)

Two pieces of 1/2-in.-by-3/4-in. pine were perfectly squared and fastened to the baseboard on both sides of the keel to support the keel at its attachment to the stempiece during construction. These pieces were separated approximately 3/8 in. in accordance with the scale width of the keel. Two small, additional 3/4-in.-by-3/4-in. pieces were constructed and fastened at right angles at the area of the stem and sternpost juncture to attempt to maintain a 90°, or right angle, orientation of the keel and sternpost with the baseboard. The squared overhead frame, or strongback with sling, was fastened to the baseboard several inches forward and aft of the bow and transom, respectively, of the model to facilitate temporary frame support as each successive frame was fastened to the keel. Keel support and overhead frame or strongback are shown in Fig. 1. The use of an overhead strongback to support and halter, or fix, the ribs or frames in place during construction will be very familiar to those who have built a dory, canoe, or small runabout vessel. The overhead frame with strongback and sling concept will also be especially familiar to those individuals who have spent any time in traction in a hospital with a fracture or other orthopedic

KEEL, STERN, STEM, AND RUDDER

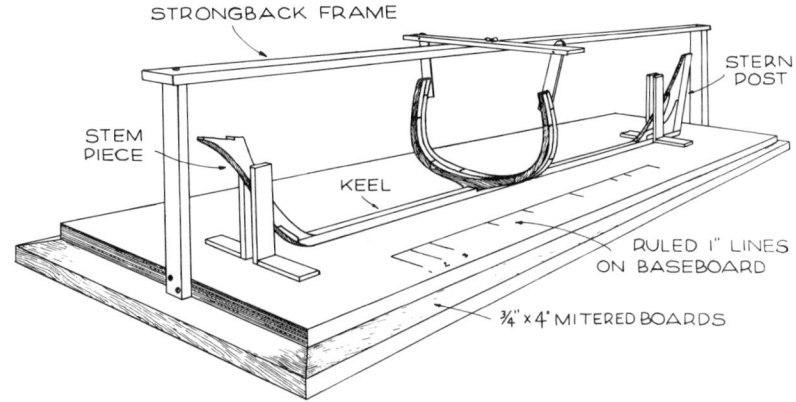

Fig. 1. Strongback baseboard

problem. One small jig which I found useful when squaring up the frames prior to fastening the ribs or frame ends to the keel was the employment of a 60° to 30° architect's plastic square preferably with measurements on one side in inches and fractions of inches which had been attached to a small wooden block 3/4 in. by 2 in. by 6 in. as shown in Fig. 2. This jury-rigged square could thus be freely moved about the baseboard and easily maintained in the erect position, more so than the thin flat edge of a grooved, movable carpenter's square. It becomes an important instrument because the final true-faired (a naval term) shape of the hull and deck surfaces are very dependent upon the initial "squared" and accurate placement of the frames or half frames on the base keel.

Whenever feasible and reasonable, all efforts should be made during construction of the model to utilize materials, especially woods,

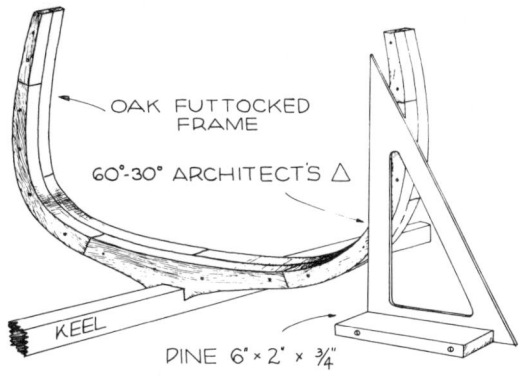

Fig. 2. Frame jig

which are identical to those used in the original construction of the *Constellation*. It should be noted that early American and British shipbuilders very quickly realized the superb shipbuilding qualities of the American white oak which was present in large virgin stands along the eastern seaboard, especially New England. Vast quantities of these sturdy white logs were shipped to England to stock their naval shipyards and to facilitate additional imperial commerce and colonization. Although not as widely mentioned, the loss of these vast American forests and their mercantile potential presented the mother country with a stimulus to quickly suppress the early cries of economic and political independence of the American colonies.

Keel, Sternpost, and Stempiece

In the model of *Constellation* all of the heavy frames, supporting timbers, keel, sternpost, stempiece, and planks were made of American white oak. This oak is strong, durable, weather resistant, and readily workable with sharp tools: in fact, it out-performs teak and shisham (shisham is a Burmese wood similar to teak but more open grained and harder, and also worm resistant) as a marine wood in most categories except for its weight per volume and susceptibility to "teredos" or sea worms to which teak is relatively immune. Also, white oak planking may be bent to the compound curves required while minimally affecting the wood's tensile strength.

The keel width on 1/4-in.-to-1-ft scale was 3/8 in., and the keel, stem, and stern deadwood pieces were all cut out with band saw to shape. Stempieces, shaped deadwood parts, and sternposts are indicated in the drawings in Figs. 3 and 4. Note also the rabbet lines and the bronze "fishplates" which were used to increase the strength of keel, stem, and stern attachments. It should be noted throughout that scale dimensions based on the 1/4-in.-to-1-ft scale are given. However, occasionally full-size dimensions will be intermittently included so that a better "feel" for the model can be obtained. This is especially helpful when the full-size measurements are known for small fittings and parts. The holding plates, called "fishplates", which attached keel to stem and sternpieces, were made from 0.04-in. brass shim sheet stock cut to size, filed smoothly, drilled, and riveted in place with small modelmaker's nails which were 3/8-in. long.

In addition to using copper or bronze bolts, the parts of the stern and deadwood oak pieces were originally fastened together by oak

KEEL, STERN, STEM, AND RUDDER

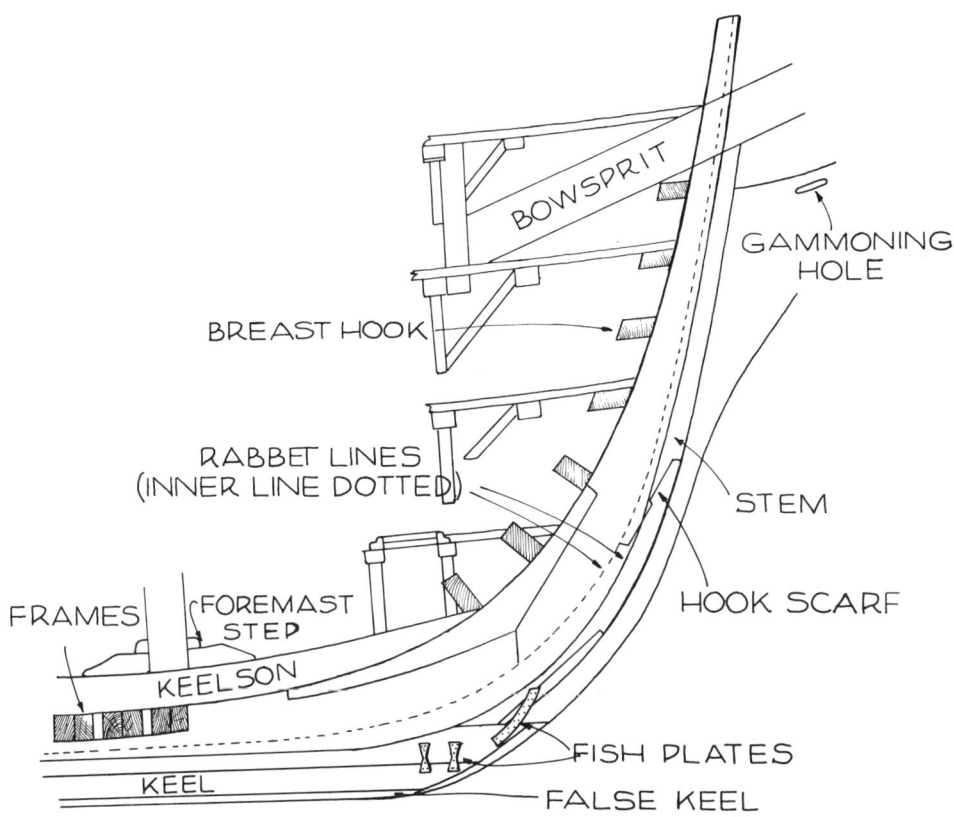

Fig. 3. Stempieces

wooden dowels called trunnels. Originally these were called tree nails, but the two words were shortened by seamen and carpenters over the years to "trunnels." The heavier pieces were drilled and attached with large, 3-in.-diameter bronze bolts and most of the trunneling was reserved for attaching the planks to the frames. Most of the deadwood pieces were tenoned and morticed prior to doweling or bolting together. The separate pieces of the keel were scarfed together in the customary sea sturdy fashion. It may be well at this time to review scarf joints. The keel joints on the *Constellation* were hook scarfed for additional wood-to-wood support as noted in Fig. 5. The various types of scarfs as shown in the drawings of Fig. 5 were also used on rails, futtocks, and planking to insure sturdy fastening and relative stability under stress.

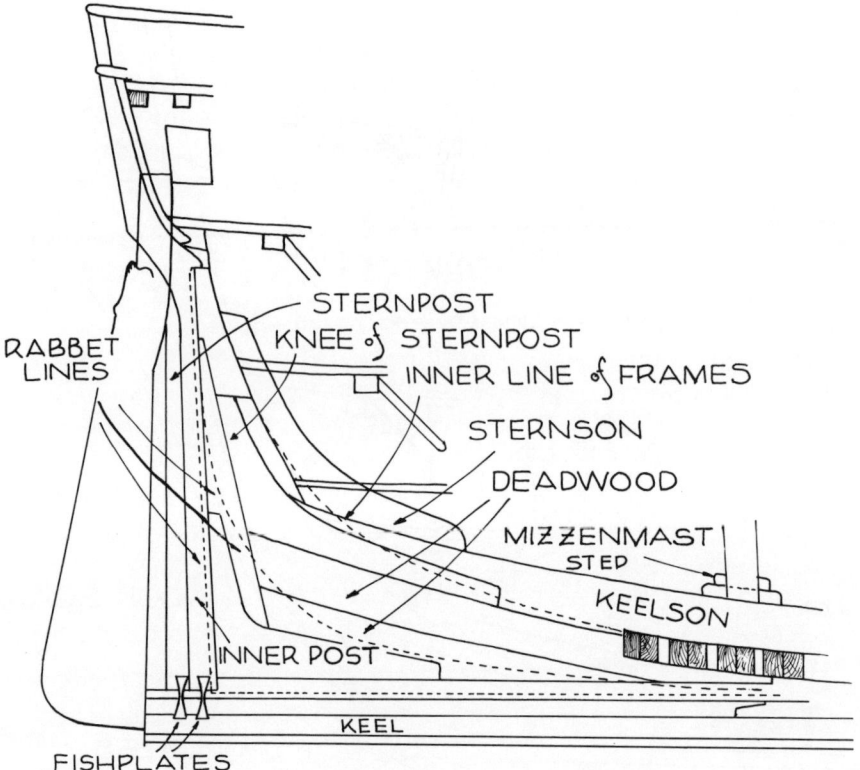

Fig. 4. Sternpost

The stern was completed after the stem apron piece and stemson were glued and trunneled together. The rabbets for the keel, stem, and stern areas were cut on the original ship before the frames were put on or the individual pieces of stem and stern were scarfed together. On the model, it is easier to determine the inner rabbet line or bearding line after the frames have been cemented and secured in place.

The sternpost and inner post were trunneled together, and then the deadwood pieces and sternson with sternpost knee were glued together. The deadwood pieces were necessary on the stern portion of the vessel because the frame pieces attach farther and farther away from the body of the keel as one proceeds aft. (This was also true of latter-day clipper ships which had a finer cut to the lower stern than frigates of the late eighteenth century—and hence more dead space.) Since the floor "rises" as one proceeds aft, the deadwood pieces were

KEEL, STERN, STEM, AND RUDDER 9

also called "rising wood". The false keel was placed on the ship near completion to prevent hogging (tendency for fore and aft sections of the boat to "sink" allowing the keel midships to be higher than stern or bow). This false keel also tends to reduce leeway according to Nepean Longridge, author of *The Anatomy of Nelson's Ships* and an authority on English ships of the line, or in other words, decreases drift to the lee when beating or reaching to windward—obviously because 6 inches more keel is 6 inches more water resistance to wind drift.

Frames

After completion of the keel, stem, and sternposts, work was begun on the frames or ribs. Each frame or rib was constructed of mutiple pieces called futtocks which were trunneled together prior to their attachment to the backbone or keel of the ship. It has been noted by many authors that there is an anthropomorphic anatomical similarity between ships and humans or animals: ribs (frames), backbones (keel), knees (breasthooks), etc. This analogy can be taken one step further in physiological similarity in that the ribs of new wooden ships are resilient and somewhat compressible just like those of a young adult. However, with age they become more brittle and hence more subject to fracture with a sudden, compressing force as with heavy seas.

Before proceeding with details about construction of the frames, several rudiments of lofting should be understood. Simply stated, a

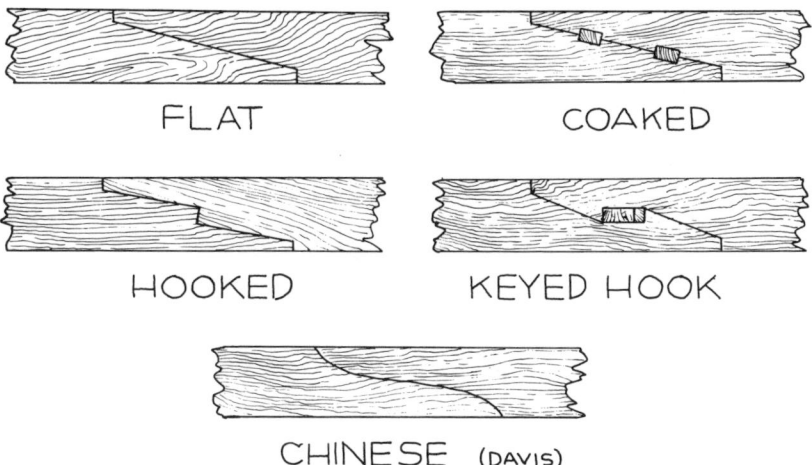

Fig. 5. Various types of scarfs

ship like any other solid object has three planes or lines: horizontal (which is water line), vertical (buttock lines), and perpendicular (which are half breadth lines, or literally half frames; or side view, top view, and end view as shown in Fig. 6. The essence of lofting then is essentially working with the end view or measuring the form of each frame from front to back or forward to aft, which determines the true shape of the ship or model of that ship. By using the half lines or the full size quarter inch plans and measuring from centerline aft and from centerline forward, each frame may be constructed of its individual pieces or futtocks. Note that each frame may be drawn from the frame shapes as presented on the body plan on Plate II.

The frames in the model were constructed in a classical manner with individual futtock pieces, trunneled or doweled together with 1/16-in. dowel as noted in Fig. 7. Most frames consisted of nine individual futtocks for each frame fashioned from 1/4-in. oak. At a specialty lumber store 1/4-in. and 3/8-in. oak stock may be purchased. If one has access to a furniture or cabinet millwork plant where such sized oak is commonly used for commercial drawer fabrication, it may be obtained from that source. The oak that I used throughout construction of the *Constellation* was obtained from 3/4-in. stock cut down to size with a small-toothed table saw. It did require some sanding to finish but obviated obtaining specially thick, individually planed boards. Several years before building the *Constellation*, I obtained from a farmer several

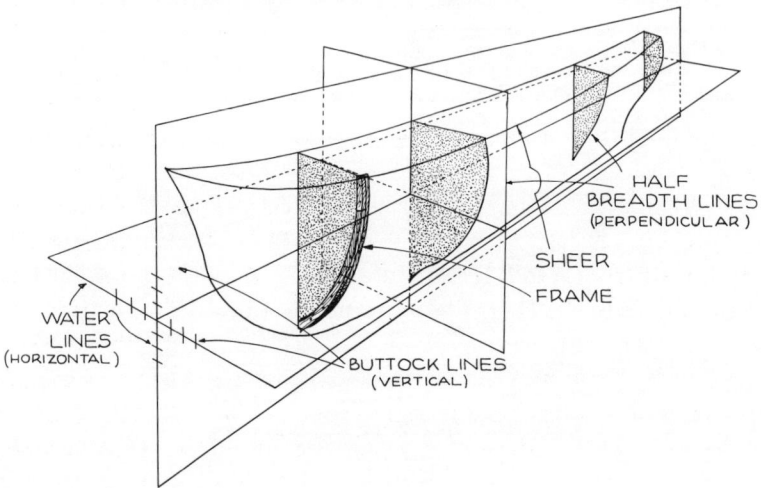

Fig. 6. Dimension planes

KEEL, STERN, STEM, AND RUDDER

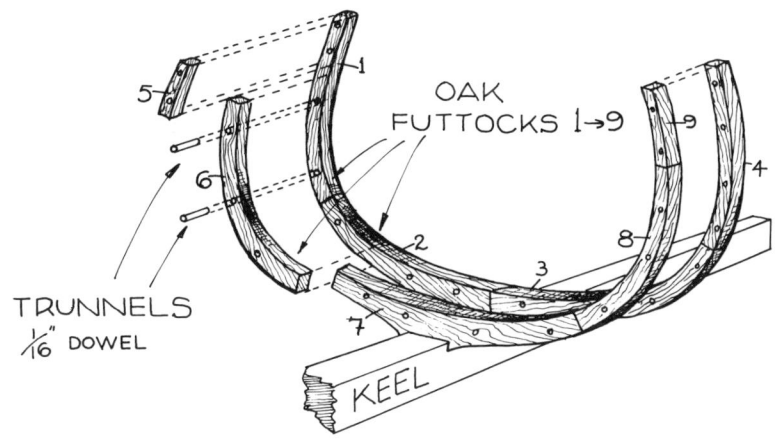

Fig. 7. Frame construction

hundred feet of rough sawn, 1-in.-thick white oak in variable widths from 6 to 14 inches. I had allowed this wood to dry in the attic prior to having it planed in a nearby planing mill. I would advise anyone planning to air dry oak planks to make sure that at least 3/4-in. small transverse wood strips or shims are placed between each plank to insure adequate circumferential drying and to prevent fungus growth between the planks. It should be noted that only several board feet of oak are needed for the entire model making the cost or the total expense of wood to complete the model from scratch very low even at the large 1/4-in.-to-1-ft scale. As noted, each futtock was cut and formed into successive frames which were subsequently attached to the backbone or keel. The frames on the keel were set up from a centerline midships both forward and aft on the vessel. Frames from A through Z and a_1, b_1, and b_2 are the frames designating forward from the arbitrary centerline, Fig. 8A. Frames 1 through 37 are the frames aft to the centerline, Fig 8B (frame drawing on Plate II.) Frames from the centerline or from A to R forward and 1 to 28 aft of the centerline were at right angles to the keel. Those frames fore and aft of the frames R and 28 respectively, were gradually canted (literally cantilevered or angled) to be more or less perpendicular to the planking sides of the ship and hence naturally increased the lateral strength of the planking timbers, and hence of the entire vessel. The futtocks were cut out with a band saw but could be just as easily cut out with a fretsaw or jigsaw, in fact, whatever saw tool the modeller wishes to purchase. (I formerly

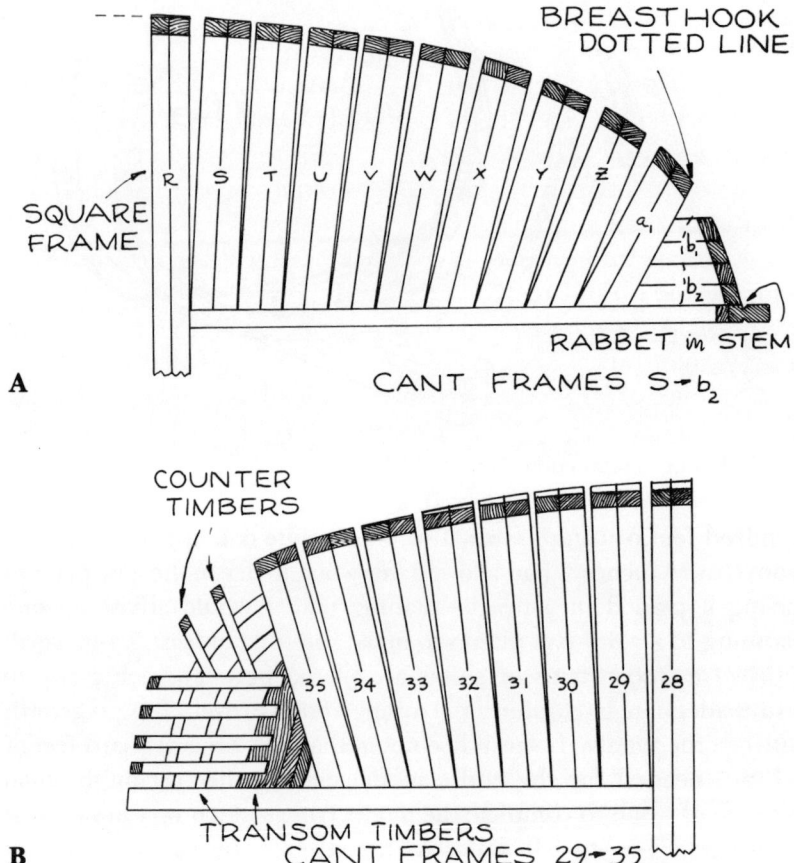

Fig. 8. Fore and aft cant frames

used a small jeweler's fretsaw and plain coping saw for model building.) Each futtock was cut out with approximately 1/32 in. or 1/16 in. extra without painstakingly attempting to taper, angle cut, or "faircut" each futtock. This is in contradistinction to Harold Underhill's method of perfectly beveling and mounting each frame after it has been partially beveled and cut. (Harold Underhill is an author of several books on plank-on-frame construction. See Bibliography.) I think it is easier in a model of this size to mount the frames partially beveled having chosen a midline frame measurement from which to bevel the frames fore and aft. This may be reasonably done from the body plan in Plate II. Once the frames have been attached to keel or backbone and stabilized, they may be faired by taper cutting them with a rasp or file thus arriving at the true faired body plan of the ship. In spite of the fact there are "purists" who state that they cut their bevels precisely before mounting them, everyone knows they end up having to do a little "fairing" themselves to get the shape of the hull uniform. Obviously it may be necessary in a large boat to taper cut the frames in accordance with the sheer of the decks and planks fore to aft. However, in a small model, this is usually unnecessary and just increases the time required to complete the rib and keel construction. In a small scale model, it is just not possible to perfectly angle or taper cut each futtock to match the concave and convex, compound curves or to completely fair up those frames which are most fore and aft of the centerline frames. It is, also, unnecessary because once all the futtocks and frames are assembled, the outer surface may be readily filed or rasped to meet the templated half-hull or half-frame shapes. Then the outer shape of each frame is faired with its contiguous neighboring frame on the outside or external surface of the hull satisfactorily, the inner shape of the hull then may be filed with riffle files or rasps and power tools so that the inner surface of the frames matches the alignment of the external surface of the boat. A Dremmel power rasp may be used for rough cutting of the inner and outer surface of the frames in attempting to fair up the hull. However, small hand sculpture riffle files and carpenter's rasps may be used very satisfactorily to form the inner and outer surface of the hull. As noted in the drawing (Fig. 7) each frame was really double in thickness for several practical reasons. First, it enabled smaller, short grain pieces of oak to be used instead of attempting to build the frame out of large curved grain oak pieces which would be difficult to obtain for the entire length of one half breadth or half a frame. Secondly, such lamination increases the functional strength of each frame.

The spacers or chocks between the perpendicular frames were 5/64 in. in size, and, although this may appear to be shaving it a bit close as far as measurement goes, each repeated piece of frame and chock, if increased significantly in size, would considerably increase the total length of the model because of the high number of frames. Similar spacing blocks of 5/64-in. thickness were also placed at the sheer line of each frame in an attempt to keep track of the measured line which would gradually become the sloping line of the entire main deck and also to facilitate accurate placement of the sheer plank. Additional or subsequent planking would have its accurate position dependent upon the initial laying down of an accurate plank sheer. To maintain the perpendicular status of the midline frames, crossbars or small temporary pieces of wood (spalls) were attached to the frames and additionally to the overhead frame or strongback to maintain frame position. After the perpendicular frames had been attached and made fast in place to the keel, the angled or canted fore and aft frames (as previously noted) from Q to b_1 and 28 to 37, respectively, were placed on the model and attached to the keel with pine spacers employed to facilitate maintenance of the increasing canted angle from the perpendicular with each successive fore and aft canted frame. The plank-sheer from stem to sternpost was then nailed to the frame with small nails to facilitate placement of the canted frames. Fig. 9 demonstrates a view of the plank-sheer in place on the fitted frames with uncut or unfinished timberheads. Also noted on this drawing are some of the spacers between frames. After the fore cant frames were put in place, the model was removed from the strongback support and placed in a small standard pine cradle to be completed.

Mounting the Frames

Each frame was glued to the keel with vinyl resin although any wood glue would suffice including white, vinyl, casein, or furniture glue. Especially good for use is Weldwood plastic vinyl resin glue which provides a good strong joint, sands well, and, although it stains more than white glue, it is somewhat stronger. These frames were also drilled in the lower midline with the keel and bolted with small, 1/16-in. threaded bolts; copper or stainless steel may be used although on the *Constellation* obviously bronze bolts were employed to fasten the frames to the keels at the midline base. After the frames were set in place with temporary spacers or chocks also in place, the temporary sheer line plank was removed and the frames shaped both inboard and outboard to conform with the smooth, taper-lofted lines of the ship as noted on the plans. Any unnatural lumps or hollows can be eyeballed by holding the ship up to a light and slowly rotating it and picking off the high points with rasp or sandpaper. Regardless of the time spent measuring the sizes of each frame in an attempt at lofting them correctly, there will be some unevenness once the frames have been assembled. Attempts should be made to smooth the ship's side and "fair it up" (in naval terms), to end up with a smooth, even, unrippled hull surface. This is somewhat difficult to describe. However, after gaining experience

KEEL, STERN, STEM, AND RUDDER

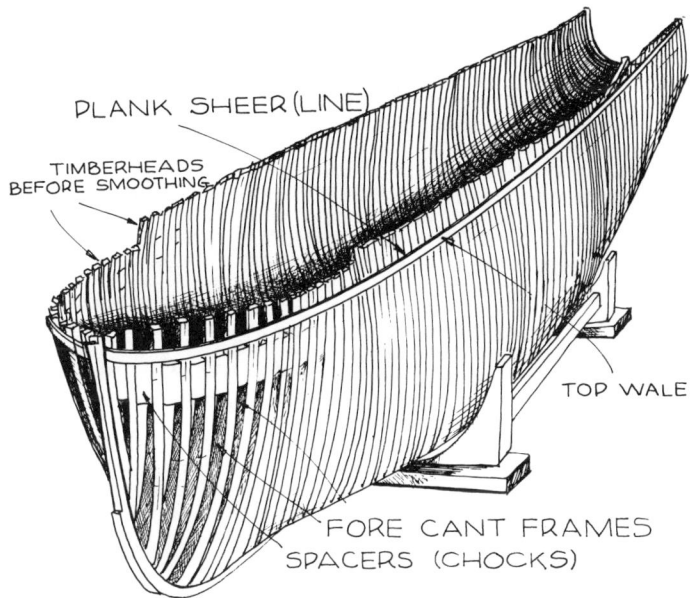

Fig. 9. Showing plank-sheer line on frame

smoothing wood and attempting to achieve good contours, it becomes instinctive, and the wood is easier to smooth in hand than it is to describe the process in words.

After the inboard and outboard frames have been shaped to the desired contours, they may be thoroughly sanded in and out commencing with #100 sandpaper and progressing to #320. There is a lot of controversy about types and grades of sandpaper to use for any sanding procedure. Flint and the old silicone sandpaper are perfectly good. When sanding hard woods, however, these sandpapers tend to degenerate very quickly, especially garnet paper, whereas aluminum oxide tends to last much longer and provides a better surface. Aluminum oxide paper is in fact manufactured for power tools because the other sandpapers do not hold a satisfactory surface for "high velocity" sanding.

Building the Transom

Once the angled or canted bow frames were glued in place with appropriate angled spacers, Fig. 10, the transom pieces were made of 1/4-in. oak, sizes as indicated on Plate II, and fastened and inserted in

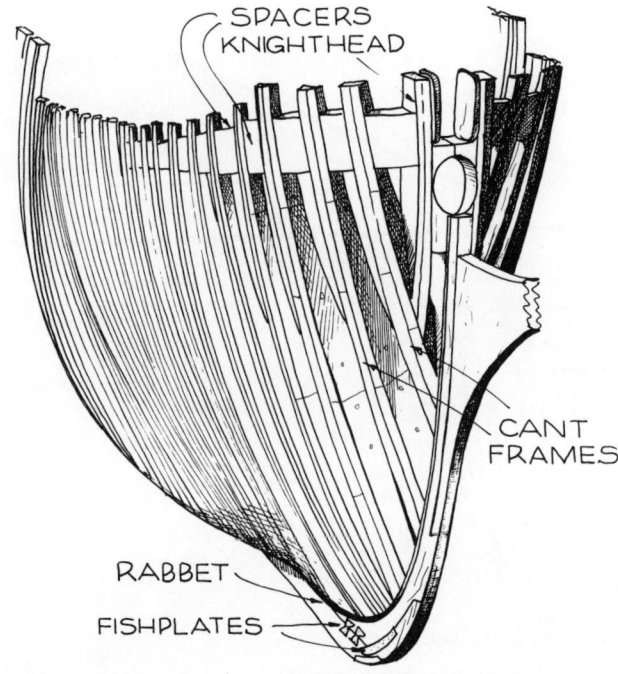

Fig. 10. Fore cant frames

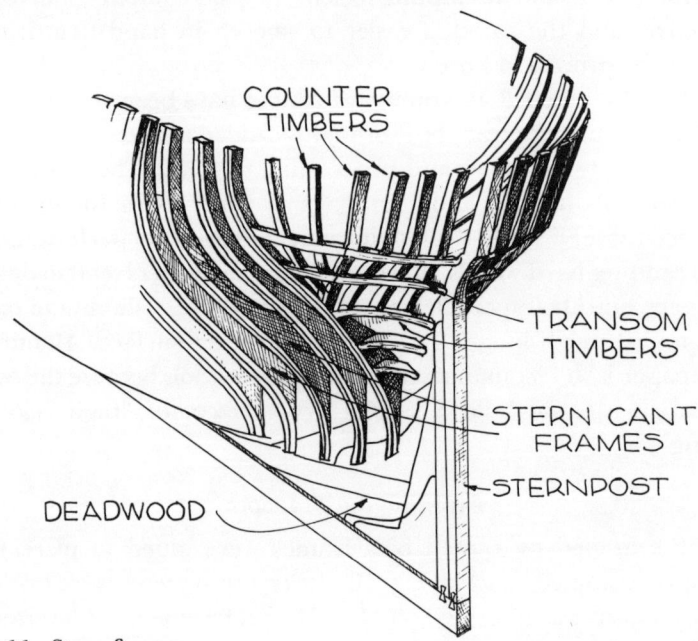

Fig. 11. Stern frames

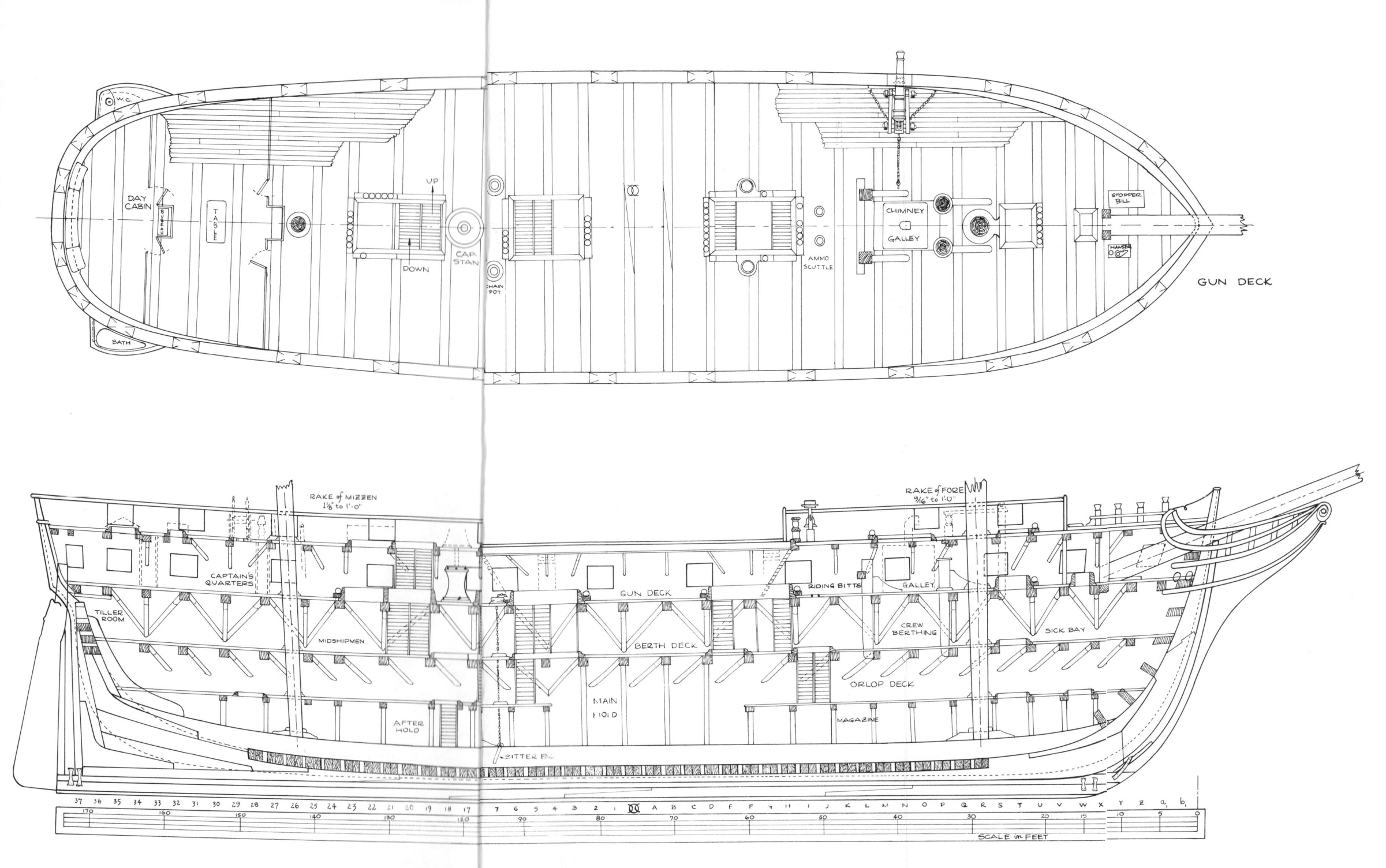
above, Gun Deck; *below*, Inboard Profile

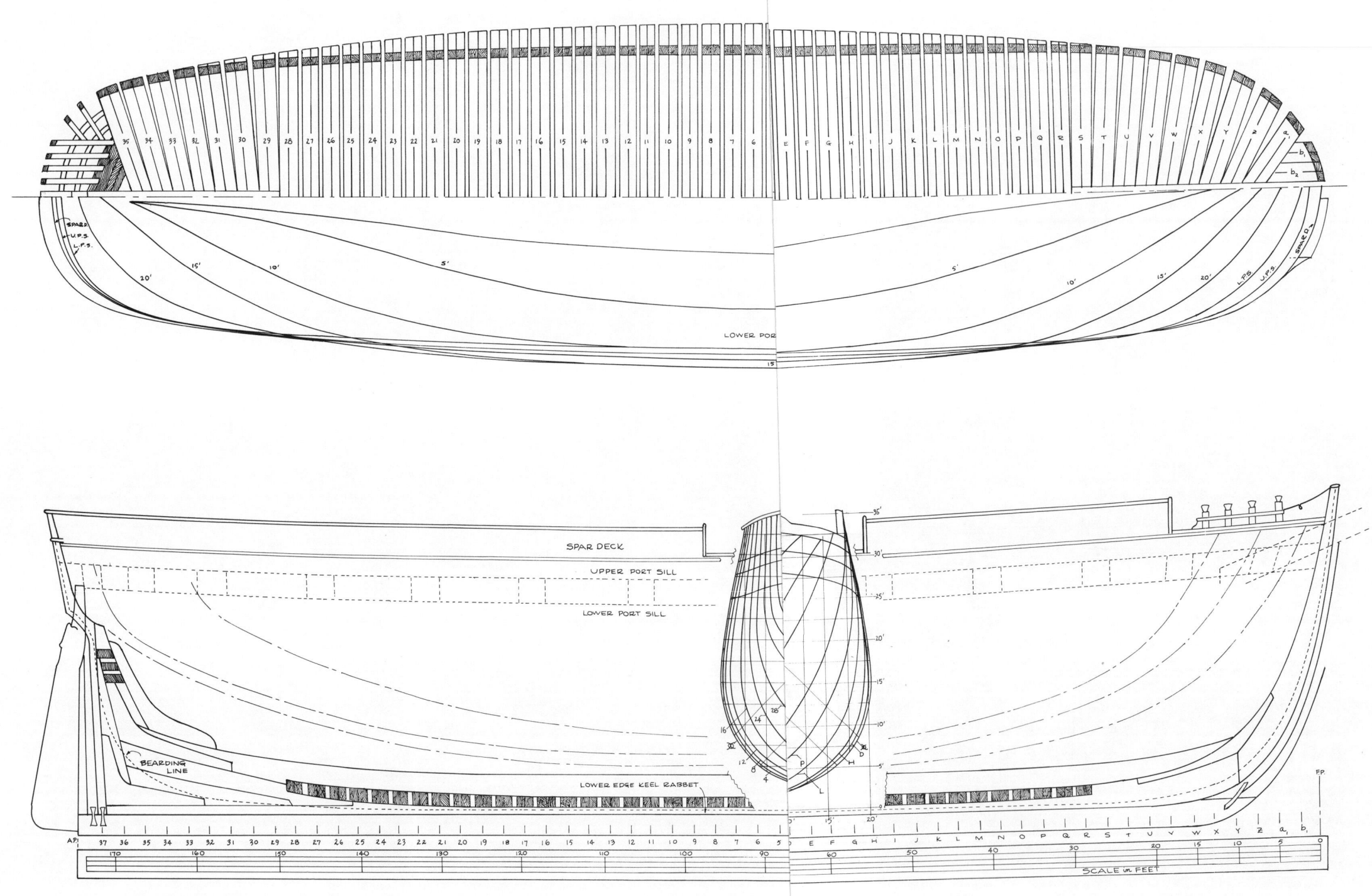

PLATE II : *Above,* Frames & Half Br'er & Body Plan

place as shown in Fig. 11. The counter timbers were fashioned according to the dimensions (size and shape of these timbers are given on Plate II) on the plans and fitted to the last canted frames as shown in Fig. 11. The transverse transom timbers, fitted across the counter timbers as also noted in Fig. 11, provided support for the counter timbers. This is especially necessary on the model as the transverse transom timbers buttressed these counter frames making them solid enough to hold against nailing and hammering home the plank trunnels through the stern planking. The "captain castles" were added on after the other deck work had been completed, and their construction will be discussed in Chapter III. The transverse and counter transom timbers may be attached with small 1/4-in. or 3/8-in. modelmaker nails in addition to gluing. Apparently, the corvette of 1853 did have a rounded contoured stern, accounting for the rounded stern appearance of the present *Constellation* (in the opinion of many the rounded stern was constructed in 1829, see Historical Notes). However, as the *Constellation* was obviously rebuilt numerous times, the better cross fire obtained from guns in a rounded stern would have been an impetus for alteration of the *Constellation's* stern upon repair at anytime after 1800. Repairs to the high stern deck superstructure above the waterline with plenty of freeboard would have been the most easily altered structural changes and, therefore, I do not think they are of great significance. On the *Constellation*, the gently rounded stern superstructure makes the quarter galleries look like "eyeballs on grasshoppers" and appear to be more added on than they do in the typical square stern vessel. In the posterior aft midline, segments of the transom beams had to be made to accommodate the rounded upper end or most of the freeboard end of the rudder. As may be seen in the present-day *Constellation*, the cover top to the rudder post is beneath the transom seats in the far aft midsection of the captain's quarters. The tiller attachment, block and tackle attachments to the wheel, are immediately below the captain's deck on the gun deck. This arrangment is obviously more convenient for the captain in that he does not have to put up with the wind and pull of the sheaved blocks attached to a tiller in the middle of his dining room. It is also to his advantage because in a far more practical sense, the captain's quarters house four of the 24-pound guns and indeed his quarters became a very active area in times of combat in that the partitions were elevated and guns were manned within his quarters.

After completion of their frames and their subsequent in-hull and out-hull shaping, the keel rabbet line was carved or grooved out of the keel, stem, and sternpost to accept the planking. This was approximately 3/32 in. in angled depth, the scale size for the oak planking which was approximately four inches thick on the original vessel. This involved removal of some of the sides of the aft deadwood pieces to accommodate the tapered rabetted lines several inches forward from the sternpost to form the aft bearding line. The bearding line is the innermost line of the rabbet line for plank attachment of the oak planks to the hull, as noted in Fig. 12.

In the midline, after smoothing of the spacers on the keel between the frames which were also 5/64 in. by 3/8 in. by 1/4 in., the keelson of 7/16-in.-by-1-in. oak was glued on the keel and bolted with several 1/16- in. bolts after being temporarily nailed in place to maintain position.

After positioning and nailing the keelson in place, the positions of the mast steps were determined by measuring from the centerline frame R for the foremast, frame 9 for the mainmast, and frame 26 for the mizzenmast. Small oak chock pieces (1/4 in. by 1/2 in. by 1/4 in.) were employed fore and aft of each mast to make and maintain the position of the mast to be stepped. These chock pieces were glued and nailed in position.

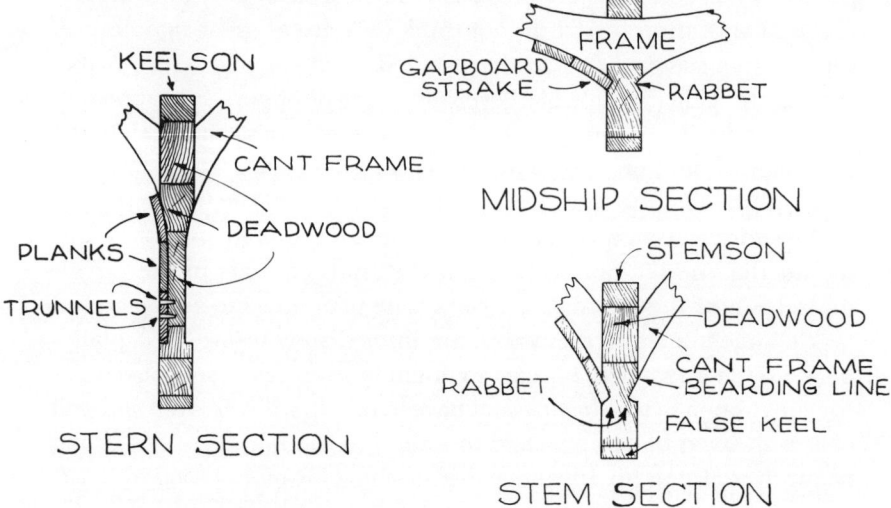

Fig. 12. Keel segments

CHAPTER II
Decks and Planking

With some ship models, it may be more reasonable to proceed directly with the planking and leave the decking, hatches, and fittings to complete after the planks are in place. However, in this instance, all of the first three decks were placed in position before completion of the planking. Of course, in a solid model or in constructing a smaller scale model of the *Constellation*, it would not be necessary to complete all of the decks other than the exposed center portion of the gun deck and the main deck. In this model, in which a moderate portion or segment of the planking and decking had been left off to display the inner structure or workings of the model, it is technically advantageous (frankly, easier to get your fingers into it) to model the deck beams and hatch coamings which are deep inside the vessel without the outboard planking in place or "in the road." With the spacers or chocks in place between each frame and the sheer strake or plank in place, the model is fairly stable and should not be torqued (twisted out of "true") or altered in shape with the motional work required to fit the deck beams in place.

The *Constellation* had four decks, from top to bottom, as follows: main deck (spar deck), gun deck, berth deck, and orlop deck as noted in Fig. ☆ (There is no Fig. 13 in this book in keeping with a superstition of the sea. My father, who was aboard a tanker which broke up in heavy seas in the Bay of Biscay on a Friday, the 13th, in September 1917, did not hesitate to incorporate into my outlook a healthy respect for the number thirteen along with such items as leprechauns and banshees.)

Except in heavy weather, the midportion of the main deck was open with small plank gangways near the gunwale or sheer line to facilitate transport on the main deck from aft to forward and vice versa. In heavy seas, hatch covers with additional tarpaulins could be placed

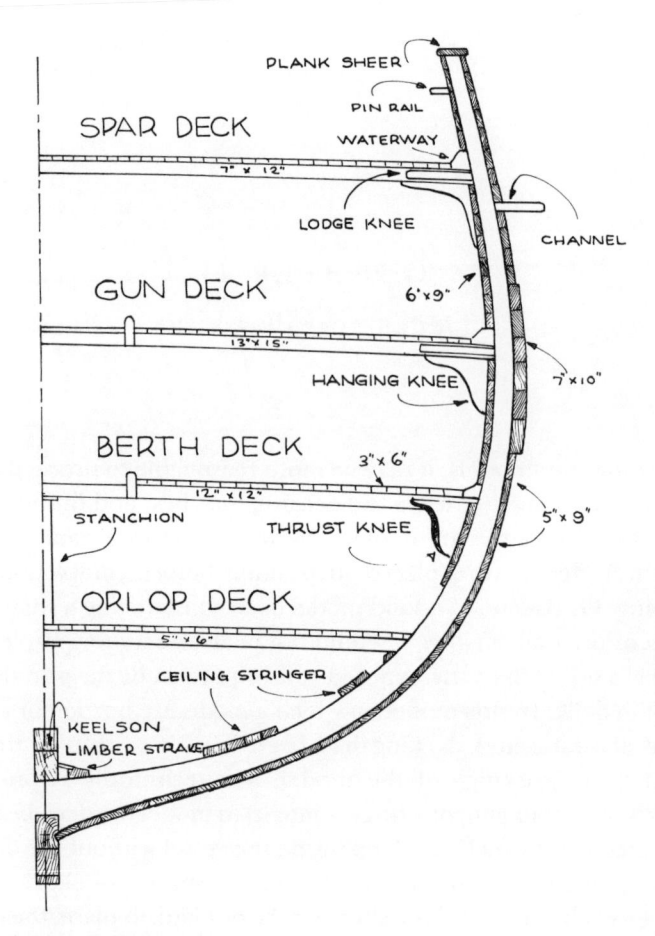

Fig. ☆. Section at frame 14

on temporary supporting beams athwartships for protection against the elements. The gun deck obviously had the main batteries and the captain's quarters. On *Constellation* guns were stationed within the captain's quarters and, when preparing for battle, the partitions separating them from the main part of the gun deck were removed from the area of combat by elevating the partitions on hinges and attaching them to the underside of the contiguous main deck beams or removing them entirely to below the orlop deck to decrease the opportunity for additional "flying" wooden splinters. (The majority of the morbid torso and extremity wounds sustained during combat were from flying wooden splinters accelerated in all directions upon impact from can-

DECKS AND PLANKING

non balls on the sides, planks, etc. of the ship.) The gun deck also had hammock positions for a goodly number of the sailors or ordinary seamen; the berth deck having separate quarters aft for the officers or midshipmen and the ship's chaplain and surgeon.

The actual practice of general medicine and surgery was extremely limited in the latter portion of the eighteenth and early nineteenth centuries. Aside from the use of a multiplicity of cathartics and poultices, the major medical duty of the ship's surgeon was to amputate extremities expeditiously after the severe splinter injuries, etc. had occurred at the time of battle. He had the ongoing respect of the crew of the ship not so much for his surgical skills as for the fact that he had sole access to the ship's stores of rum—which by necessity was the only form of surgical anesthesia available. He was, therefore, held in high regard in spite of any aberrances of personality. If a seaman was unfortunate to receive a chest or abdominal injury of any magnitude, he would be sure to die as the surgeon was practically helpless to prevent the ensuing inevitable mortality.

Forward, as one might expect in the most unpleasant area of the damp cold ship, were the open bunks and hammocks for the seamen. The orlop deck did not run the entire length of the original ship (or the model for that matter); its center section was incomplete leaving an open area called the main hold. It was the area where food stores, cordage, spare spars, sails, carpenters' supplies, water, grog, and the boarded up or separated magazines where the shot and powder were placed and stored near where the shot pots were located. These pots were holes in the deck surrounded by a metal or hardwood frame where the cannon-shot was relayed up from one deck to another during battle. There were several small boarded up areas on both sides of the keel and keelson where the ship's ballast, which was usually pig iron and brick, was positioned—although obviously these were not placed on the model. The deck beams of the original vessel were made up of several large beams or lengths of heavy oak planks which were scarfed together and then cut or adzed to obtain their cambered shape. The camber was approximately 1/8 in. to 1/4 in. per ft, and this "slow" curve enabled the water to easily run off the decks and through the scuppers and into the sea. The gentle sheered lines of the various decks of the model were made by utilizing a small jig which was constructed to facilitate obtaining the sheer of the decks which, by the way, was coincident with the outboard planking. The ultimate curve of the spar deck, placed at the level of this deck, was identically sloped with the original sheer plank. As noted, the upper edge of each frame spacer had been placed at the sheer strake or plank line to facilitate placement and subsequent outboard plankings thereafter, including the spar or main deck. An inner wale along each side of the frame or ultimate position of the main deck waterway was temporarily nailed with 1/4-in. flathead nails to the bulwark, exactly parallel to the outside sheer stake line. From the side view of the ship, a measurement was taken of the distance from this inner wale to the top of the orlop deck beam which was approximately 3-1/4 in., as shown in Fig. 14.

Deck Beams

A small, transverse beam or piece of wood, approximately 1/8-in. in thickness to fit in the space between each frame, was placed on the inner wale between two frames and a 3-in.-long block of pine cut to the dimension of the distance from the wale and the top of the orlop deck minus half of the diameter of a pencil (3/16 in.). Thus, the width of the block was 5-1/16 in. A pencil was then taped to the block of wood, and, by altering the position of the jig between successive frames from bow to stern, the sheered line of the orlop deck was progressively drawn on the inner surface of the frames. A similar method was employed to determine the placement of each additional deck, obviously altering the size of the small wood block to compare with the measured distance for each deck from the wale to the top of each successive deck beam. Several bellystringers or wales were placed midway between the orlop

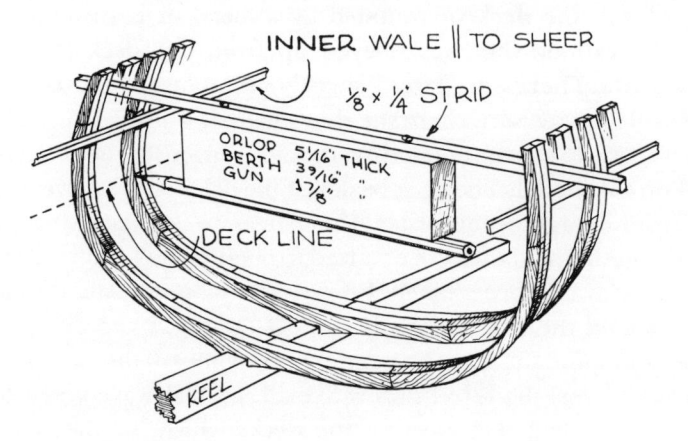

Fig. 14. Jig for deck lines

deck and the keel. These were made out of 3/32-in.-by-1/4-in. oak wood. By placing a small piece of wood between each frame, an accurately measured and scored length of a deck beam could be determined and direct measurement transferred to an oak piece which could then be cut to size for each individual deck beam piece, as noted in Fig. 15. The beam thickness, as will be discussed later, varied in proportion to the stress upon each deck; obviously the gun deck, having more stress than the other decks, had heavier beams. On the original *Constellation*, these deck beams were angle cut to match the frames and then bolted in place with bronze or copper bolts. These bolts were not similar to the bolts that are currently utilized in that they were not threaded but the ends were placed through holes in metal plates and then clenched or hammered over these plates for rigidity and permanent fastening. The obvious difficulty with these plates is that if the bolt end fractured, the plate had to be recessed more deeply into the wood which weakened the frames. The beams, from frame 8 aft and frame H forward of the centerline in the midportion of the spar deck (see Plates I and II), were not in place on the original vessel which facilitated storage of heavy materials directly to the gun deck or through hatches to the berth deck from the wharf thus obviating transport from spar deck to gun deck. Each beam had appropriate knees or cross supports to maintain its stability with the frames, the exception being the orlop deck in which cross knees were not utilized. After completion of the orlop deck, the berth deck slope was measured from the height of the inner wale with the aforementioned jig and an

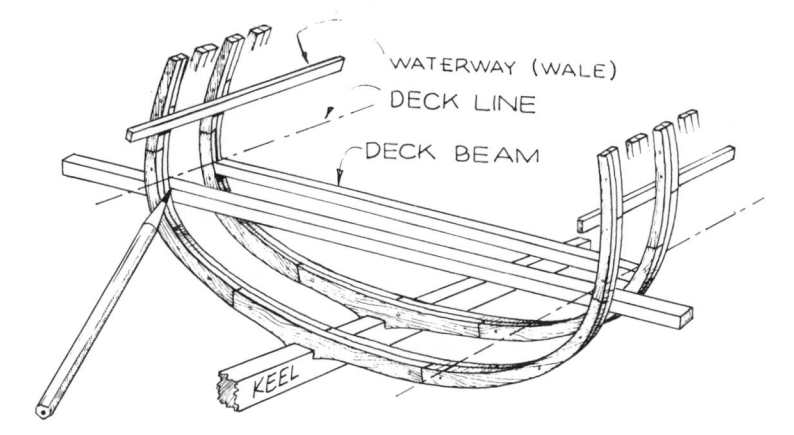

Fig. 15. Measuring deck beams

appropriate line marked off on the innerside of the frames to coincide with the slope of the berth deck. The width of the next three deck beams was maintained at approximately 1/4 in., although the thickness of each beam varied depending on the stress placed upon the deck as stated previously. The gun deck beams were 13 in. by 15-1/2 in., obviously based on the fact that this deck had to support heavy 24-pound gun carriages and associated shot. This dimension proved to be very close to the scale of 1/4 in. which is a conveniently measured size of oak to cut and sand smooth.

Knees

All of the individual compartments of the midshipmen with their attendant bunks and the details of the orlop deck were not placed on the model as these details could not be significantly displayed and would, in any case, be almost completely obscured by the above captain's quarters and main deck even without the maindeck and gundeck planking in place. Therefore, detail was reserved for that deck which could be adequately displayed with some convenience especially the specific details of the gun deck and main deck. After each berth deck beam had been measured and cut to fit, it was fastened and glued in place and the appropriate knees were placed at each beam. The types of knees made at the beam frame junctions of the berth deck are called thrust or daggar knees and are at a 45° angle with the perpendicular, as sketched in Fig. 16. The other types of knees employed to reinforce attachment of deck beams to frames in addition to the thrust knees or daggar knees are hanging and lodge knees. The hanging knees were at a 90° angle to the deck beams and the lodge knees were on the same plane as the deck planking itself or, in other words, parallel to the sea. Lodge knees and hanging knees are illustrated in Fig. 17.

Most of the knees in wooden ships were made of the roots of hackmatack, tamarack, or larch. Very large knees were occasionally made from the crotch or notches of large oak trees and other hard woods if hackmatack was not available. The reasons for utilizing these segments or portions of trees were to take advantage of the normal prestressed or curved nature of the grain and its inherent strength. Any compressive force or torque forces applied to the beams and subsequently the knees could be more advantageously used to counteract these forces by using curved grain knees as shown in Fig. 18. Shipments of maple, hackmatack, white oak, and white pine were

DECKS AND PLANKING 25

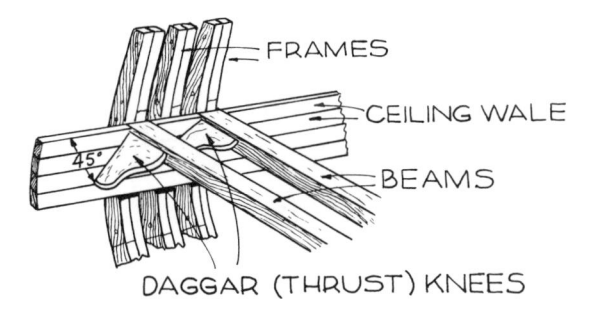

Fig. 16. Daggar knees

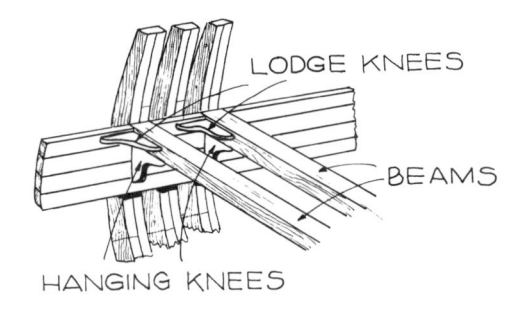

Fig. 17. Two types of knees

made from New England to the eastern seaboard states before 1750 and, therefore, were available in Maryland. Additionally, curved grain oak from the crotch of the tree and the roots of large locust trees make good knees, and locust is abundant in Maryland. With reference to the orlop deck the knees were present in the berth decks of the *Constellation, Constitution, Congress,* and in the English ships of the line including the *HMS Victory.*

At any rate, the knees in the model were constructed of 1/8-in. oak with the exception of the hanging and daggar knees for the main deck or spar deck gangway which were made out of 1/32-in.-thick white basswood to prevent the splitting which occasionally occurs with thin oak pieces of wood. Prior to installation of the deck beams of the main deck or gun deck, the hatches, of 3/16-in.-by-5/16-in. oak and basswood were installed for the orlop and berth deck as noted in Fig. 19. There were six hatches in the orlop and six hatches on the berth decks constructed and fashioned as noted. The notched hatch covers for these hatches were not placed in so that the model viewer can see

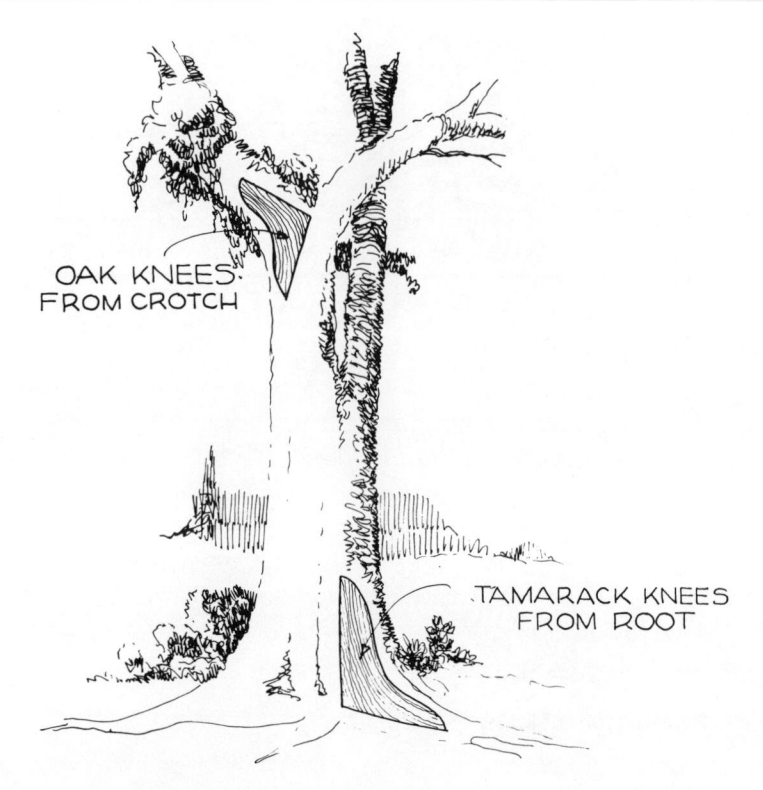

Fig. 18. Knees of hackmatack

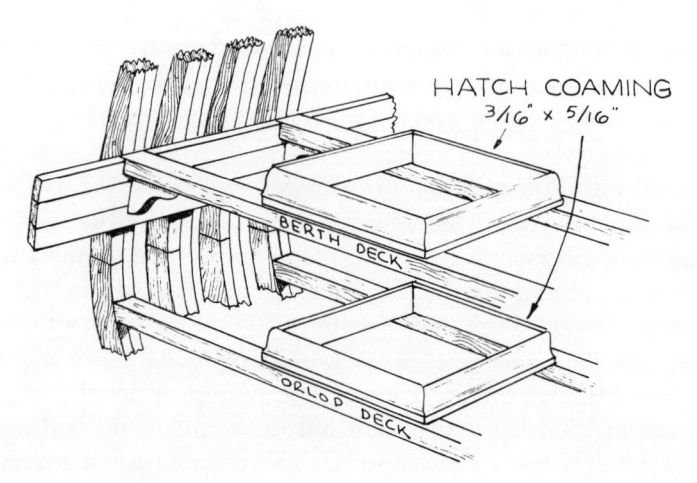

Fig. 19. Hatch construction

DECKS AND PLANKING 27

between decks. The decking of the midline of the berth deck for the approximate width of the main hatch was utilized to demonstrate the decking but not entirely to obscure the hold or the orlop deck below. As noted in the plans (Plates I and II), the beams from station centerline aft to frame 4 and forward from centerline to frame F of the orlop deck were not in place; in their stead were midship stanchions which supported the berth deck beams from the keel or riding keelson; this is also noted in Fig. 20. These stanchions were fashioned out of 3/16-in. oak or rock maple dowel which was turned and fashioned to shape prior to installation beneath these berth deck beams.

Breasthooks were fashioned for each respective area of the bow of the ship from 1/8-in. basswood and oak and glued in place as noted in Fig. 21. These added significantly to the strength of the bow as they were in the athwartship direction and, also, facilitated anchoring of the planking in the bow and cutwater area of the ship. As the angle of the breasthook progressively became more acute with the keelson, each successive breasthook was fastened at approximately right angles with the rabbetted keel. There were breasthooks stationed between each deck forward.

Waterways

After completing the gluing and attaching of the orlop, berth, and gun deck beams, including appropriate thrust knees of the berth deck, waterways were constructed for the gun deck out of beech, as noted in Fig. 22, and nailed in place about the periphery of the gun deck. In the original vessel, the waterways were constructed out of adzed and

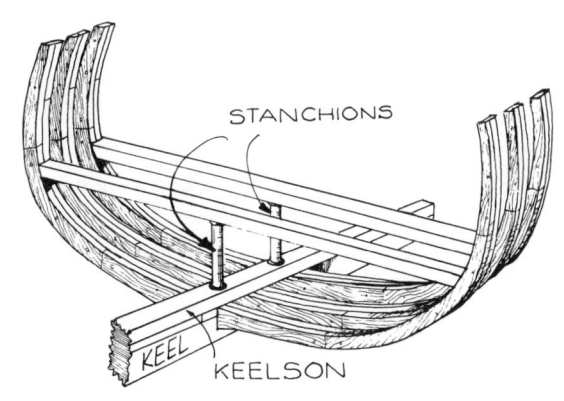

Fig. 20. Lower deck stanchions

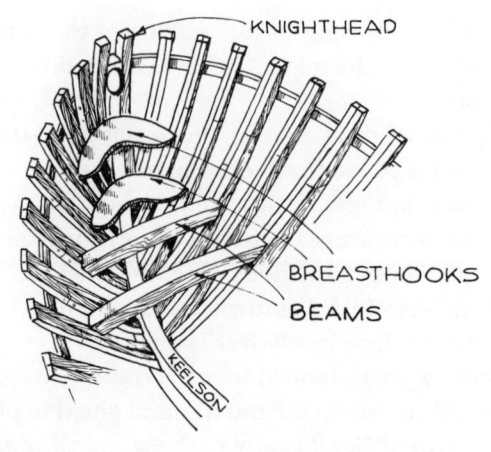

Fig. 21. Breasthooks

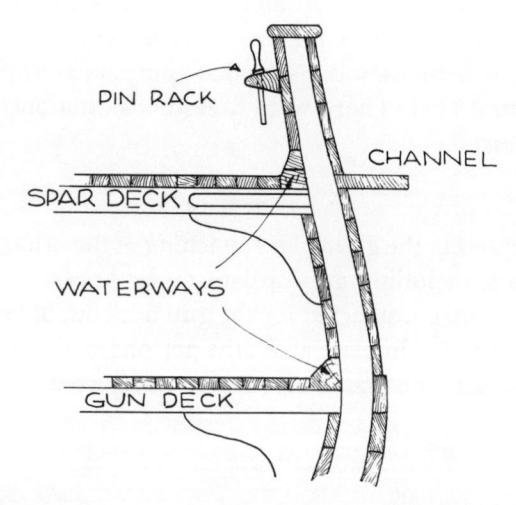

Fig. 22. Waterways

hewed oak, approximately 9 in. by 10 in. and beveled to fit the contour of the decks and bulwarks. I employed beech in the model which was, also, similarly employed on many whaleboats because of the acute angles needed in order to construct a smoothly curved, satisfactory waterway. Beechwood, 7/16 in. by 3/16 in., was utilized as it is extremely malleable and easy to bend and accommodate the compound curves of the deck-bulwark junctions especially of the forecastle and stern or transom. These beech pieces were tapered to match the contours of the side bulwarks and inserted on the gun deck beams and then nailed in place. Holes were drilled in the waterways to serve as scuppers through which water would be allowed to run off the deck into the sea.

Planking

When sufficient work had been done "in the depths" of the model ship, it was possible to proceed with the planking of the outboard section of the ship. The greater part of the planking of the *Constellation* was fashioned from selected pieces of white oak, 3 in. by 9 in., steamed, bent, and trunneled in place. For the model, because of the attendant problem of splitting and checking when working with such small pieces as necessary, I made the only significant substitution in wood types in that I used 1/4-in.-by-3/32-in. basswood for ship planking. The basswood is a close grain unlike the open grain of oak and, therefore, somewhat more compressible, fitting the contours of the forecastle, canted frames, and the acutely angled stern more easily on a model than would be necessary on a full-size *Constellation*. I had always envisioned using applewood for the frames as had been used by the fantastic wooden ship modelist, John Crabtree, but although I had some small applewood trunks at the time I made the model, I didn't have any sufficiently dried out to cut for planking. Mr. Crabtree and others state that applewood is the best wood to use for models, especially for planking and small-scale carving.

Fastening the Planks

As noted in Chapter I the method of fastening the oak planking to the *Constellation* was to stagger trunnels which had been made from oak and placed into the frames and to supplement them with bronze nails which were clenched over end plates. To simulate these copper fittings, copper and stainless steel nails were employed on the model to hold the planks in position for trunneling with small oak pegs; this facilitated plank placement and, also, significantly eased the difficulty in placing the basswood planking down with merely oak pegs for maintaining position prior to completing the planking. The oak pegs or trunnels were placed in drilled holes into the frames and wales similar to the method that was employed on the original vessel. They were staggered from the top of one plank to the bottom of another plank on the nearby or adjoining frame in order to prevent splitting of the planks. The only difference was that on the original trunnels, small transverse oak pegs were placed inside to impact them into the oak or wooden nails as noted in Fig. 23. This done on scale with the model would not be visible as it would be less than 1/128 in. in diameter, therefore, not practically possible to simulate. On the seagoing *Constellation,* the wooden pegs were extemely useful because unlike bronze or iron fittings they would not rust out. Furthermore, the oak trunnels would swell within their drilled areas after taking on water and become watertight and extremely stable and difficult to move. With the exception of the persistent sea worm damage, they had a similar life span as that of their adjoining oak frame and plank structures. As shown in Fig. 24, the trunnels were staggered and altered in placement so as not to weaken the plank and increase strength to lateral and torque motion of the hull. As it is difficult to obtain a 1/32 in. dowel, I, therefore, utilized 1/32-in.-by-1/32-in. oak stripwood, either basswood or oak which had been pulled through or extruded through a 1/32-in. hole previously drilled in a piece of hard metal. The metal need not be extremely hard; I used a piece of scrap zinc-plated or galvanized stove duct which had a hole drilled and tapered to that diameter which served very well for this purpose. At first glance, it would seem difficult to obtain a round dowel through such a small hole with a very small piece of wood, however, once the end of the wood is passed through the hole, it may be pulled very readily through this hole several times making a perfect 1/32-in.-round dowel which will correspond to the size of the drilled hole in the plank. To insure an accurate fit with such small trunnels, the same drill which I used to drill the metal was used to drill holes in the planking and frames. The holes may be drilled readily with 1/32-in.

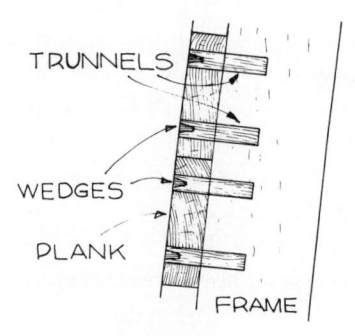

Fig. 23. Trunnels

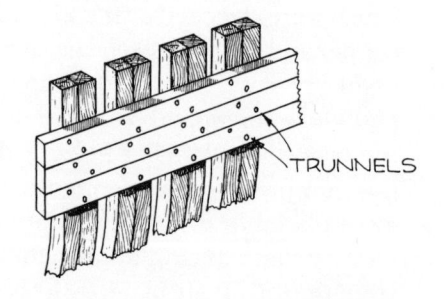

Fig. 24. Plank fastening scheme

DECKS AND PLANKING

drill placed in the pin vise, although a high speed Dremmel-type drill, preferably with a flexible shaft attachment, can speed up the process considerably and lessen the rather long time it takes to do each piece by hand as there are several thousand trunnels necessary even with the planned limited planking of the model.

The first plank permanently fastened to the frames after the temporary one had been removed was the sheer plank. It was shaped to fit the stempiece rabbet and then nailed and trunneled in place. As this strake conforms to the gradual sheer of the deck, and serves as the guiding plank or permanent plank from which the remainder of the upper and lower planking from the sheer line is accomplished, it should be accurately placed. For the girdlings or thickened armored areas of the planks, approximately six planks of 1/8-in.-by-1/4-in. wood were utilized to conform to the heavily planked area of the man-of-war instead of the 3/32-in. thickness employed for the remainder of the planks. As previously mentioned, with the exception of the garboard strake or the lowest plank on the keel rabbet, the lower one-third of the planking was not placed on the model in order to enable the viewer to visualize the interior construction details, particularly, the deck and cabin areas.

In the stern area, the marked concavity and the greater distance to be covered by the planking necessitated use of planks called stealers, and two of the commonly employed types are noted in Fig. 25 along with cross-sectional views of the girdlings and garboard strake in place on the rabbetted keel. Fig. 26 demonstrates the specific or special manner in which the planking was altered to accomplish the satisfac-

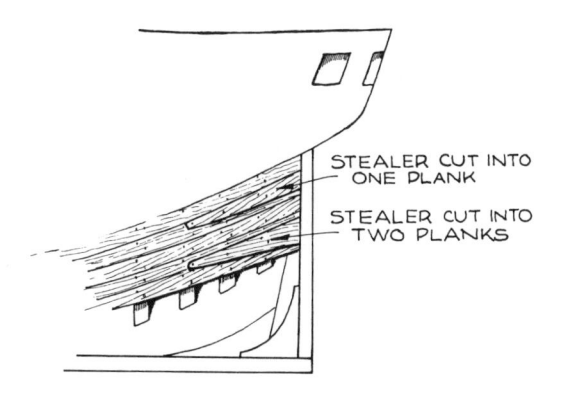

Fig. 25. Plank "stealers"

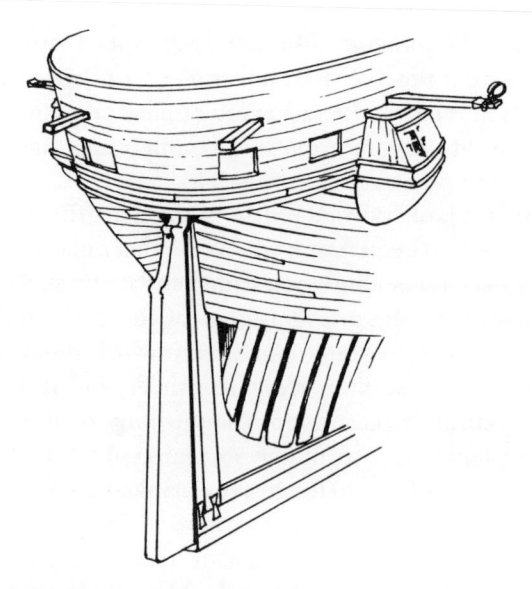

Fig. 26. Transom planking

tory covering of the marked curve of the planked area below the transom and at the area of the inboard part of the rudder.

The final planks placed or fastened to the frames were those above the sheer or gunwale. In the transom, these were steamed and bent to accomplish the compound curve of the transom in addition to its angle with the deck. There are a number of ways or methods which can be employed to steam the transom planks. The initial one which I used was to place several 1/4-in.-by-3/32-in. wood planks or strips over a large metal pot (home canning size) on the stove and allow the steam to permeate the wood for subsequent bending. As this method proved somewhat slow, I then advanced to the simple expediency of holding the five or six strips at a time under hot water, bending them to shape and then placing them between two, prefashioned or preshaped wooden molds in the shape of the transom and allowing them to dry prior to adding to the model (similar to the old-time method of bending and holding in place with straight pins, either bamboo, beech, or balsa for the wing tips of stick-model airplanes). Although I have never used them, there are commercial frame-bending tools which may be purchased and utilized at one's discretion.

After completing the framing, a hole was drilled in the inferior aspect or underside of the stern to accommodate the rudder post. The rudder was then fashioned to shape from 3/8-in. thick oak plank, tapered to 1/4 in. at the aft or trailing edge of the rudder and then attached to the hull with small gudgeons and pintles. The pintles and gudgeons were made from 0.0018 shim brass which had been cut to 1/8 in. width, drilled with 0.62-in. drills, and then nailed in place with small modelmaker's 1/4-in. brass roundhead nails obtained from James Bliss and Company, a supplier in Boston. Small pins were used in the notched area of the rudder to form the pintle attachment to hold the rudder in place. A small 1/8-in.-by-1/8-in. hole was drilled in the upper inside part of the rudder post and squared (morticed) to accommodate the end of the tiller which was constructed from 1/8-in.-by-1/8 in.-by-3-in. oak. The tiller and oak rudder are as noted along with their pintle and gudgeon attachments in Fig. 27. The method by which the tiller was rigged to the steering wheel will be discussed in Chapter III.

It should be noted that there are other methods of attaching the planking to the hull and any homemade frame clamps could be used,

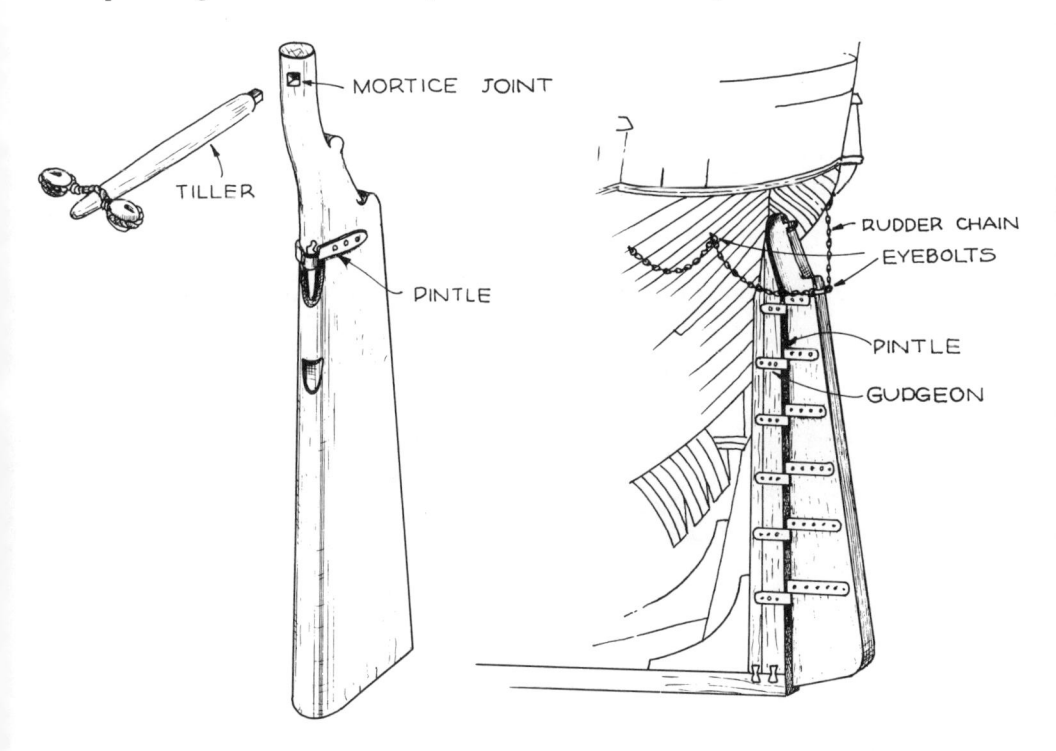

Fig. 27. Tiller and rudder

one of which is illustrated in Fig. 28. For those that wish to glue the planking in place prior to using the trunnels, a small homemade clamp made from 1/4-in.-by-1-in.-by-3/4-in. pine, held together with 1/16-in. bolts could be utilized to hold the planks in place on the frames to allow the glue to dry. After drying, the trunnels could be subsequently drilled and glued or impacted in place with a small, modelmaker's hammer.

After completion of the stern and outboard planking, the next planking to be added was that of the ceiling wales or inner gunwales which were fashioned and nailed in place. Again, as previously noted with some of the outer planking, several of the ceiling wales or inner planking were left off the model to insure the model viewer the opportunity to view the method of construction of the frames, deck beams, and thrust beam attachments. The ceiling wales were not placed on the model below the berth deck and, therefore, the thrust knees of the berth deck beams were attached to the contiguous frames instead of the wales. However, above the gun deck, all of the ceiling wales and bulwark planking including those above the main deck were completed before cutting out the areas needed for the gunports. Some of the planking of the inner surface of the stern bulwark had to be tapered in order to accommodate the obtuse angle intimately associated with the deck bulwark slope.

Placing the Gunports

After completion of the inner and outer planking, measurements were

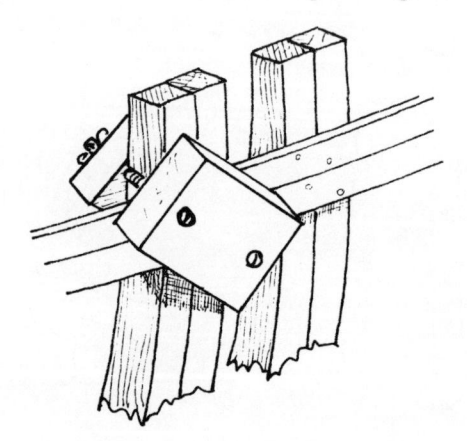

Fig. 28. Simple plank jig

then taken to determine the placement of the gun ports. Some modelists would prefer to measure the dimensions for placing the sides of each gunport and cut the planking to accommodate these areas as the model planking process progressed. I used that process in the plank-on-frame models of the HMS *Victory* but changed with this model as the height of the gunport seemed to be more accurately determined for placement of the top and bottom gunport sills after the planking had been trunneled and nailed in place. It is obviously true that if one were to construct morticed sills for the upper and lower borders of each gunport as noted in Fig. 29, it would be impossible to fashion these sills in situ or in place with the planks including the ceiling planks or inner wales in place. However, with the model, the proper placement of these sills is cosmetically dependent on each plank position, and, although each plank width could be measured from the sheer plank to determine its exact placement, minor alterations in this measurement and slight unseen changes in the alternating frames would make the final port sill placement not readily in line and hence detract from the pleasing appearance of the nicely shaped gunports closely following the plank lines. The sills were, therefore, placed after the exact size of the port had been measured and cut out. These sills were cut flush with the sides of the port and frame and glued in place with epoxy or vinyl resin glue to assure their permanent placement. The size of the gunport was determined on the original vessel by the old-time naval architect's standard rule based on the size of the gunshot. The gunports

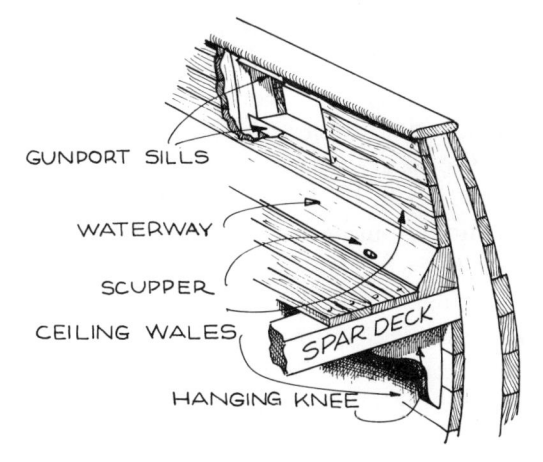

Fig. 29. Gunport sills

were, therefore, separated from each other, center to center, by 25 times the diameter of the shot; at 6.5 times the diameter for fore and aft length; and at 3.5 times the diameter for the lower ceiling edge above the deck. This method works well on a large vessel, however, on a model one is attempting always to keep things ship-shape and pleasing to the eye. Therefore, it is advisable to spend the time accurately measuring the placement of the gunports as it will save many hours of frustration later on when the vessel is being rigged.

Mast Steps

The safest way to proceed at this point in building the model is to determine mast placement which will enable one to determine the position of the channels and chain plates for the placement of the deadeyes because obviously one cannot have chain plates or any other gear running in front of the gunports. This will, also, serve as a double check for satisfactory frame and mast placement when it is done. The mast steps were placed in position after being marked prior to insertion of the orlop deck. Using the centerline and the slope or rake or each mast, the rake of the mainmast being 3/4 in. to 1 ft, the foremast rake 9/16 in. to 1 ft, and the rake of the mizzen mast 1-1/8 in. to 1 ft, the position of each mast to the main deck was determined in the following manner: the end of a 2-ft section of a 1/2-in. dowel was placed on the forepart of each mast step at the keel between the orlop and gun deck beams. The marking of 1-ft above the deck of the bulwark or rail line was made on this dowel and using a carpenter's 1-ft square and a 2-ft level, the slope at 1 ft was measured and the approximate line noted and drawn across each beam bulwark even with the front of each mast as noted in Fig. 30. With this temporary dowel in place, the front border of each mast could be marked at the spar and gun deck level and from this line the accurate position of the gunports in relation to the mast and frames could be determined, measured, and marked. Prior to the final cutting out of the gunports, the angle of the chain plates and shrouds to each mast was estimated to assure additionally not placing any rigging structures in front of the gunports. With the height and slope of each mast known, the angle of the shrouds with the mast could be determined and the gunports accurately placed. Approximate size of the gunports was 7/8 in. by 3/4 in. with approximately 2-1/2 in. between each gunport with the exception of those near the mizzenmast which were closer together or approximately 2 in. apart. See Plates I and II.

DECKS AND PLANKING

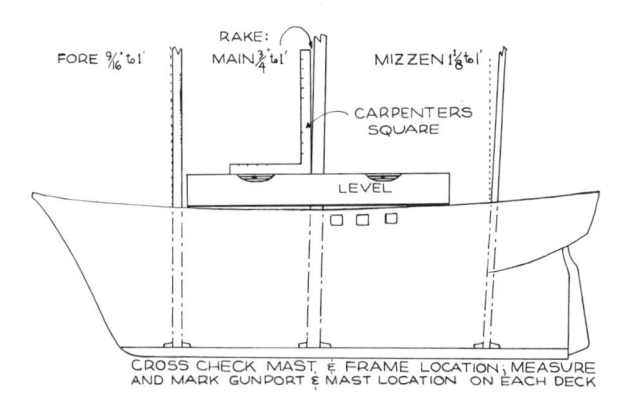

Fig. 30. Mast and gunport position

Making the Gunports

Once the gunports had been marked with pencil on the outer planks, the easiest way to carve their shape is to incise perpendicular lines on the sides with a sharp pointed knife or scalpel to prevent splitting and then drill out the center section of each gunport with 3/8-in. drill, preferably a metal drill as there is less splintering. The remaining or extra wood that has to be removed to square and fair up may be done with progressively smaller drills advancing to triangular files, needle files, and small blocked sandpaper to smoothly finished off the edges. After the gunports were cut out, the upper and lower sills were glued in place out of 1/8-in. or 1/4-in. thick oak or basswood stripping. These can be finished off and smoothed down as just mentioned for the sides of the gunports.

After completion of the gunports, the top timbers or timberheads of the frames were filed and smoothed off with the upper planks to be equally distant above the deck or sheer line. This is greatly facilitated if the upper wale is in place instead of merely measuring from the sheer strake to the top of the frame. In other words, the frames may be cut off even with the most upper wale and smoothed and faired off with a large file which will run across both bulwarks at a time assuring that they are parallel with the deck. It should be noted that the timberheads vary in height particularly in the midship area of the spar deck gangway where they were only several inches above the main or spar deck waterway which would be approximately 1/16-in. on the model. These run from frame H forward of the centerline and frame 8 aft of the centerline. Also, the timberheads forward of frame Y are at the bulwark level in the bow of the ship. Construction of the final portions of the knightheads, hawse pieces, and forward canted frames and timberheads will be discussed in Chapter III.

We have now completed the following on the model: keel, frames, outer planking, partial ceiling planking, rudder, gunports, mast steps, orlop, berth, and gun deck beams with some planking on the center portion of the orlop and berth decks. It is now necessary to complete the fittings on the gun deck along with the captain's quarters before construction of the spar or main deck. Obviously, it would be very difficult to mount the tackles and hold the carriages of the 24-pound guns in place while working through the deck beams and decking of the main deck. The main deck line was, therefore, not constructed until the gun deck was almost completed.

Painting Specific Areas

In order to obtain a pleasing, painted finish for those parts of the model requiring painting, it is necessary at this juncture to paint several areas before proceeding, specifically the gun ports and the ceiling wales of the gun deck and main deck. The gun deck inner planking, and bulwark planking above the main deck were painted flat white. The paint used was white pigmented shellac, although white enamel would probably be slightly more durable, because it gives a nice, warm, opaque color with matt finish after several coats and has minimal lap and run tendencies. The shellac may also be easily thinned with wood alcohol and brush care is simplified. The bulwark wales of the spar deck were painted with this white finish, however, using three coats to obtain the desired finish. Before the application of white pigmented shellac, I gave the frames, keel, and lower deck beams two coats of plain shellac for a natural finish. The areas to be painted white were also sealed with several coats of plain shellac prior to painting. The reason that I chose plain or orange shellac is that it gives a smooth natural finish without the "piling up" that occurs with varnish, especially the polyurethane varieties. Although shellac is less water resistant, this characteristic is not necessary on the model. Also, the shellac penetrates and seals the open grain oak without leading to the eventual cracking, fracture, and opacity which occur with the old-time spar varnish resin finishes. It is easily applied, dries quickly and, therefore, facilitates work that is interrupted frequently. Small areas may thus be

DECKS AND PLANKING

painted and immediately worked on, which is more difficult with slow-drying varnishes as you have to wait for them to dry before proceeding.

The stern windows were painted white at the time of the painting of the ceiling planking of the stern bulwarks. The stern windows were made from small bamboo pieces glued together inside the frame which was the same size as the gunports, 7/8-in. long-by-3/4-in. wide as noted in Fig. 31. There were nine smaller windows constructed of 1/32-in. split bamboo, glued in position, and painted white before installation into the port. In this particular model, the window glass was left out during the construction period as it tends to become dusty or scratched and obscures the inner view of the model. Many substances could be used to mimic the glass, for example, isinglass or cellular Plexiglas. Plain glass could be used but it is more difficult to install than the plastic materials as they are more readily cut and glued in position. The gunports and ceiling wales of the gun deck were painted red on the *Constellation* as they were on most men-of-war whether English, French, or American. The inner surface of the gun deck and the gun carriages were painted red on many ships of the line. However, on this model in order to preserve a glimpse of the method of ceiling wale construction, the gun carriages and deck were left natural but were covered with several coats of shellac. In my model, I chose to paint roughly one quarter of the stern part of the gun deck bulwark with a slightly darkened flat red. I used Tester's model flat red enamel, approximately 1/100 parts red to one part black, which provides sufficient darkening to decrease the white highlights of the standard model red. The sills and sides of all gun ports of the gun deck were painted red also.

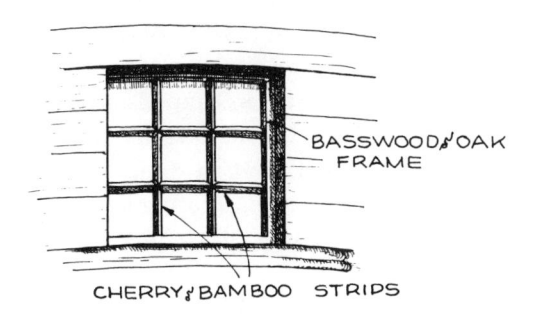

Fig. 31. Stern windows

Although the reader may be aware of the reason for painting the gun deck (or decks of the men-of-war) vessels red, it deserves repeating here. At times of combat, the metal or cannister shot would splinter the wooden timbers of the ship causing many severe wounds and lacerations which would bleed copiously. In order to decrease the psychological stress caused by the sight of so much blood on the seamen, deck, ceiling, and ancillary equipment, were painted red. As the decks would also become slippery, it was the duty of the shotboy (who passed cannon shot from the magazine to the gun deck) periodically to empty buckets of sand on them to prevent additional injury to seamen from slipping on the blood. When spending a Friday or Saturday night in the Emergency Room caring for car accident victims, I sometimes wonder what the hospital administrators would think of painting the Emergency Room floors and walls red.

The other important point that should be made about painting models in progress is that certain parts of the model should be painted while the building process is going on. For example, a much nicer line can be obtained if a natural-finished beech waterway is nailed against a previously painted bulwark, and one does not have to contend with attempting to strip paint a finely painted line, all the time worrying that paint may inadvertently be placed in the wrong area or spilled into an area not to be painted. It is, therefore, advisable to paint certain areas and fittings of the boat while in progress and while the parts are apart to avoid painstakingly painting fittings after the detailed parts are glued together in place, and, obviously, technically more difficult to reach. For some modelists, this may present no problem. I am still attempting to rid myself of the old habit acquired when making stick-model airplanes of after having everything made and glued in place to relish the final painting as the last thing to be done. Not so with model shipmaking; the last thing to be done is usually something like placing a small piece of running rigging on the gaff boom. One additional point should be made in regard to the well timed and planned painting of the model. Any metal, for example, mast bands, or wood finishes that need to be painted in the model are best done, if possible, prior to their assembly as it gives a clean, nice, pleasing look to the model and once again saves time in the long run.

Gunport Lids

Before discussing the completion of the remaining portion of the gunports, specifically the gunport lids, I should say several words about

DECKS AND PLANKING

the deck planking on the orlop and berth decks which was mentioned without detail earlier. Between the open hatches, approximately 1-1/2-in. wide segment of each deck was planked in the midsection with 1/8-in.-by-1/16-in. oak or basswood planking. This served to give some continuity to the decks without obscuring the view of the beams, frames, knees, etc., from the upper decks.

The gunport lids were constructed from laminated pieces of 1/4-in.-by-3/32-in. basswood and oak strips similar to the gunport lid construction on the original vessel. The outer layer was parallel to the outer planks and the inner layer was perpendicular or at right angles to this outer layer as noted in Fig. 32. The gunport lids were painted prior to attaching metal fittings and hinges to obtain a cleaner job. The inner surface and edges were painted red and the outer surface flat black to blend with the eventual flat black of most of the hull on the waterside as well as to accentuate the black gunport lids strategically placed in the ship's "white stripe."

Small pieces of 1/16-in.-by-1/32-in. basswood with rounded edges were glued and nailed between the upper border on the outer bulwark between the gunports. Above each gunport and in continuity with this section of wale or stripping piece, a fitted section of piano wire, 0.03 in. in diameter, was cut and fit in place to which was attached the gunport lid hinges. An illustration of these hinges is noted in Fig. 33(A) along with a segment of the outer stripping or wale above the gunport, shaped like an inverted V. This was obviously a decorative feature from the Greek Revival architectural style. In addition to the one-piece gunport lids, the foremost and aftmost of the gunports were in two sections with double eyebolts on the lower sections—their construction is as noted in Fig. 33.

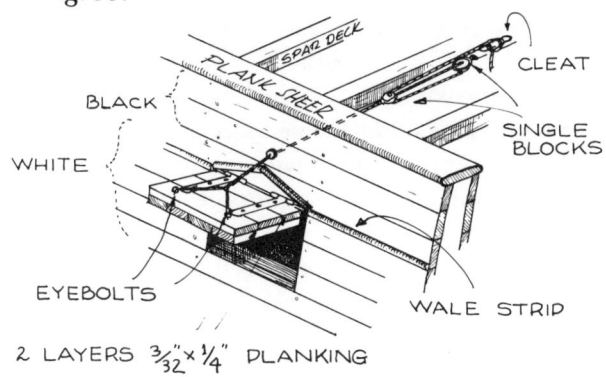

Fig. 32. Gunports

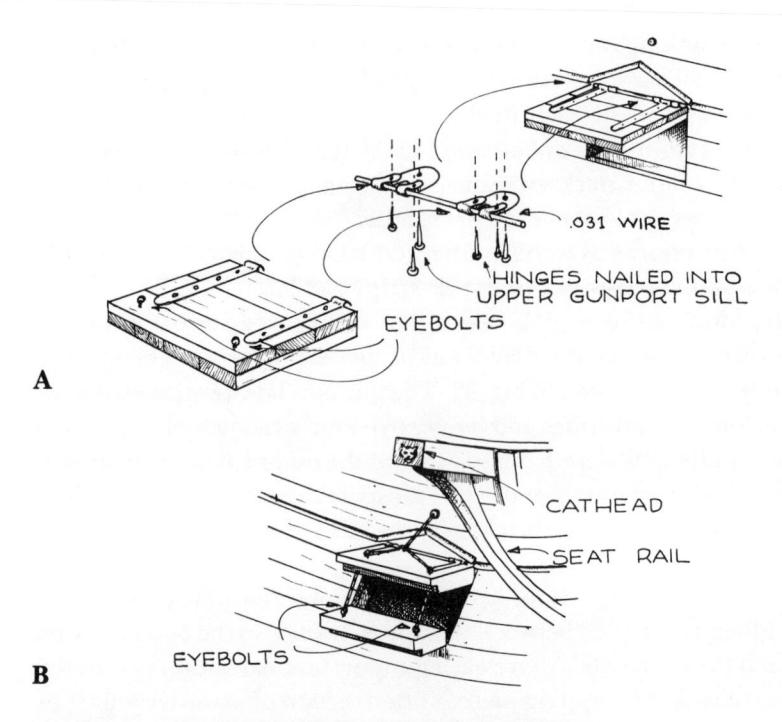

Fig. 33. Gunport hinges, (A), and a split gunport, (B)

The model hinges were constructed of small, cut pieces of shim brass, approximately 1/16 in. wide, drilled, and then attached to the gunport lid and upper gunport sill with small 1/4-in. brass escutcheon nails. These nails, along with small packets of shim brass of varying fractions of an inch in thickness, may be obtained from most hobby shops, especially those that have model railroad supplies. Above each port at 3/8 in., a 1/16-in. drill hole was made. The fairlead for each rope to the gunport lid was made in the following manner: a small piece of 1/16-in. dowel approximately 3/16 in. long was drilled with a .060 drill. This hole served as the fairlead hole for the rope. One end of this small dowel piece was gently rounded with sandpaper. 1/16-in. holes were drilled in the planking above the gunport lids into which these small drilled dowel pieces were inserted. The rope was subsequently seized to a single block. A second rope seized also to this block was then reeved through another single block which had been fixed to a spar deck beam. The fall was then looped to a nearby cleat. These two features are included in Fig. 32 but obviously the rope and its gunport lid elevation tackle cannot be completed until the spar deck beams have been in place. Construction of the spar deck will be taken up in Chapter III, after completion of the fittings on the gun deck.

Additionally, before the gunport lids and hinges were attached to the hull, the outer wide strip of painting was completed as this particular area was also obviously more easily painted before the gunport lids were installed. The gunports were sequentially spaced in one "white stripe" along the length of the ship.

Much has been written about the historical evolution of the use of the white stripe on war vessels of the eighteenth and nineteenth centuries with arguments advanced about which period the stripe was white and which period it was yellow ochre. The HMS *Victory*, as presently preserved, has a yellow ochre stripe apparently because in 1765 the English Admiralty in accordance with Admiral Nelson's wishes decided that was the way it was to be. Therefore, some historians refer to this yellow stripe as "Nelson's stripe." I decided to paint the stripe white since my research indicated that at the time of the Revolutionary War, it was white on most of the U.S. frigates. Some of the controversy may stem from the fact that the paint was leadbased and, although oxides of lead may be yellowish-white, the paint may have contained yellow or orange iron oxide impurities which in sufficient quantities develop a faded yellow cast, especially with exposure to sun or ultraviolet light. Incidentally, titanium oxide white paint does not yellow or fade with time or exposure to the elements and can be used to determine certain ages of oil paintings. Anyway, without further digression, a flat white stripe was painted on the hull and the hinged, gunport lids were attached and preparations made to complete the gun deck fittings.

PART II

FITTINGS

CHAPTER III
Stern Section, Quarter Galleries, and Forward Timberheads

Parts of the hull that I consider for construction in this chapter are the stern section, captain's castles or quarter galleries, and the forward timberheads including bowsprit, stem scroll, and hawser holes—which should be completed and painted prior to consideration of mast and spar construction and rigging of the vessel. The fittings of the gun deck were completed for convenience of construction before placing the spar deck beams in place. The inner bulwarks of the captain's quarters and aft of the previously-painted-red gun deck bulwark and the inner wales of the bulwark above the potential spar deck area were painted with flat white paint identical to the outboard, gunport white stripe. The painting of this area before the spar deck beams were in place considerably eased the painting problem of the captain's quarters, bulwarks, and stern.

Hatch Ladders

The fitting items to be completed first were the hatch ladders between the gun deck and the berth deck, and they were constructed as noted in Fig. 34(A). Small pieces of basswood or oak wood, 1/16 in. by 1/8 in. were used as the sides (styles) of the ladders, angle notched to receive the ladder rungs (treads) which were constructed parallel to the deck of 1/8-in.-by-1/32-in. basswood strips. The remaining ladders of the vessel were patterned and constructed in a manner similar to this. The rope bannisters or railings were constructed of small, tea-yellowed linen line threaded through 1/8-in.-by-1/16-in. wooden posts as noted in Fig. 34(B). Each ladder was given several coats of shellac prior to being glued in place, and work was begun on the captain's quarters.

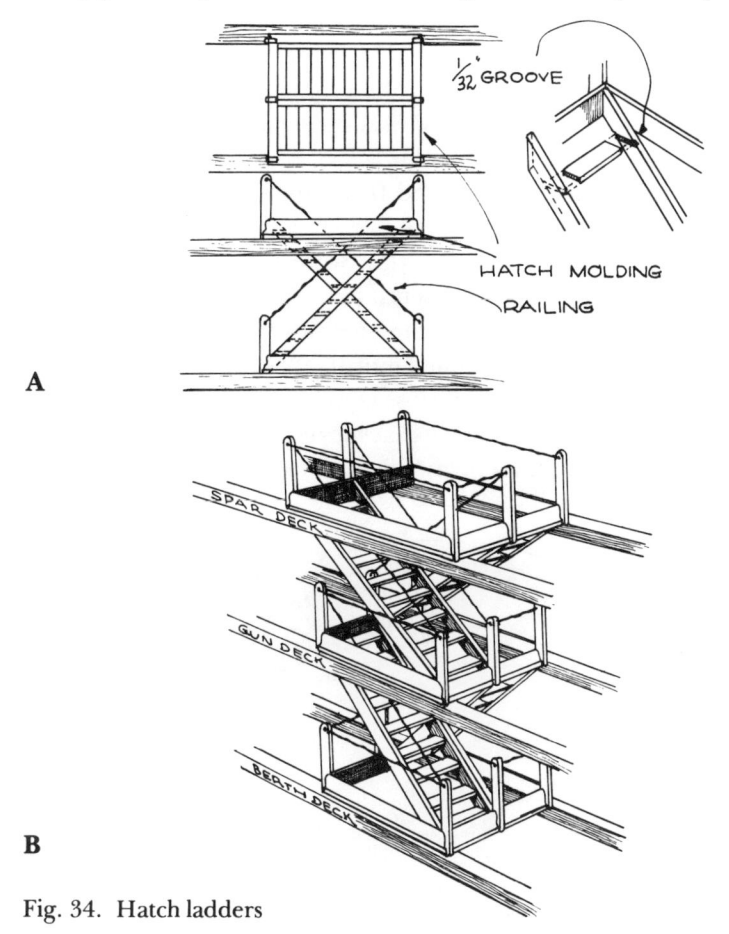

Fig. 34. Hatch ladders

Captain's Castles or Quarter Galleries

The essential items to be considered in construction of the captain's quarters, exclusive of the gun carriages discussed later, are the captain's "castles" or quarter galleries, the latrine, benches, chair, table, chest, and trunk. Although the present USF *Constellation* at Baltimore's Inner Harbor has a chain-suspended bunk for the captain's bed, I did not include it on the model. Two of the aft side window ports, which had been cut out previously, were utilized as access to the captain's privy; walnut, cherry, or mahogany folding panels could be placed on the sides of the entrance to the gallery. These shutters were constructed as indicated in Fig. 35 and, on this particular model, were constructed of wild cherry stock and morticed walnut with small 1/16-in.-by-1/32-in. walnut pieces with the total panel size 1/4 in. by 3/4 in. approximately. These panels were held together with small wire hinges to simulate the morticed hinges on the original vessel. The captain's castles or quarter gallery or "privy" was constructed of multiple cabinet-sized planks and frames on the larger vessel. However, on the model, each section was constructed from small pieces of solid wood which were mounted on the vessel's side after the outboard planking had been placed in situ. These "castles" were actually historical remnants of European vessels of the tenth to the twelfth centuries, especially cogs and carracks, in which the bow and stern simulated castles with turrets constructed or mounted inordinately high to gain mechanical advantage when engaged in close combat with other vessels. The greater height was an advantage in that spears and other missiles could be more readily cast to the enemy's deck. This was to continue as an

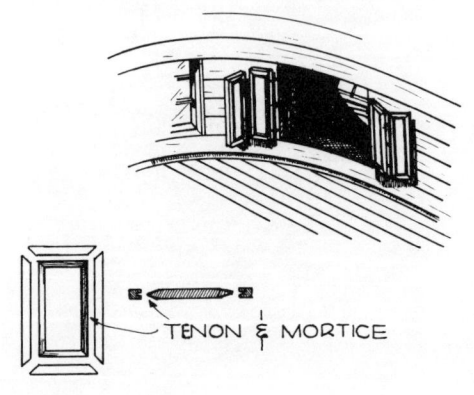

Fig. 35. Quarter gallery panels

STERN SECTION, QUARTER GALLERIES, FORWARD TIMBERHEADS 47

inherent construction feature of sailing vessels for many centuries, although obviously so much freeboard sacrificed seaworthiness especially when sailing to windward. Anyway, the dimensions and characteristics of the captain's quarter galleries are as noted in Fig. 36 with the side view shown in Fig. 37. The captain's "tub" was zinc or lead and served as the location of an infrequent cold water bath and head. Although not comparable to the comforts of present vessels, the captain's toilet was sumptuous and private when compared with the regular seaman's open bowsprit privy. On the model's section, the lower part of the gallery was hollowed out of a single piece of oak, 2 in. by 1 in. by 3/4 in., and the inner section hollowed out and covered with a small shim of lead to simulate the tub. The side windows were constructed as were the stern windows from small beech or 1/32-in. bamboo strips for window frames. The sides and roof of the gallery were constructed of 1/4-in-by-3/32-in. planks, similar in size to the regular planking of the

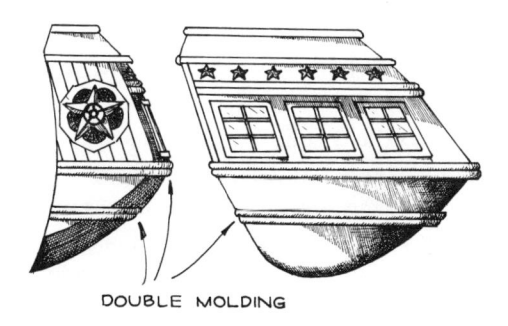

Fig. 36. Quarter gallery

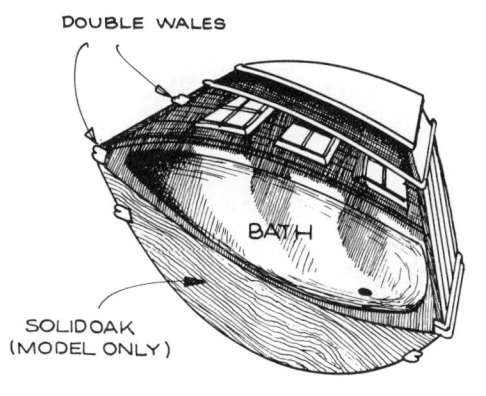

Fig. 37. Quarter gallery (inside)

major frames. The stars between the upper wales of the quarter galleries were fashioned from small, 3/16-in.-by-1/16-in. tin brass pieces filed in a star-angled shape as noted. The aft starburst was made from a small, 1/32-in. oak plank (model airplane 3-plywood firing wall will also serve well as a base) cut in octagonal shape. The star was cut out of cherry wood, and the five firebursts from the side angles of the star were constructed from shim red Plexiglas. To be more authentic, the starburst could also be constructed of cherry veneer and painted red. These small pieces were glued onto the octagonal base which was subsequently glued on to the stern and aft linearly planked area of the quarter galleries. The small, curved wales on the sides of the quarter gallery continued about the entire stern and were constructed of small pieces of beech, 1/8 in. by 3/32 in. size with a small groove cut in the midline of the flat surface to simulate double beaded coaming as shown in the quarter gallery or stern drawings (Figs. 36, 37, and 38). After having been painted flat white and flat black as noted, the galleries and planking were mounted with small modelmaker's nails and glued to the side of each appropriate stern area. The outer window frames were painted flat white to match the white gunport strip of the ship. It should be noted that the metal stars and aft starburst were not glued in place until these sections had been painted flat black. The flat black paint, which was utilized both to paint the captain's quarters and the remainder of the vessel, was Sherwin-Williams flat black. Over the years, I have tried many types of flat blacks but find that they do not remain flat, and vary in the consistency and quality of their "flatness" with occasional shiny highlights. Therefore, I prefer the old-fashioned flat black which dries very slowly, but gives a nice, soft, uniform, consistent surface which is very pleasing to the eye.

Outboard Stern Details

I added the remainder of the stern details after painting the stern section, specifically, the window frames and contiguous strip, flat white and the remaining exposed planking flat black. The lower planked section of the model was not painted flat black all the way to the waterline in order to preserve for the viewer the method of trunneled plank construction. This method was carried out the length of the vessel with only several planks below the white stripe painted black. This maintained a normal curve parallel to the plank sheer and was not a straight parallel waterline like the normal waterline. The middle transom starburst was constructed identically to the starbursts of the stern sections of the quarter galleries as detailed in Fig. 38. The wide-curved stern section, to which the aft starburst was attached, is also noted in Fig. 38, and was constructed of double cherry wood veneer although thin plywood would also readily suffice for its construction. It was nailed in place with small 3/8-in. or 1/4-in. flat head steel nails into the underlying transom planks of the stern after being painted white.

The eagle was carved from wild cherry (applewood or boxwood would be just as satisfactory) as it was on the original vessel and then gold or gild painted. The model eagle's dimensions were 2-5/8 in. by 7/8 in., and it was mounted with two small brass nails drilled through each wing as shown in Fig. 38. The main brace bumpkins which were mounted over the captain's quarter galleries were fashioned from 1-1/2-in.-by-1/4-in.-by-3/8-in. oak, beveled and rounded at each end to which a large, single main brace block was mounted as indicated in Fig. 39. The wale molding, which transversely crossed the stern, was double beaded or molded as noted (also in Fig. 39). The molding was epoxied and nailed in place as was the stern bumpkin except that the stern bumpkin was morticed approximately 1/2 in. into the stern frames prior to being epoxied in place. The two were painted flat white. The stern davits, constructed from 1/4-in. square oak, were inserted through a drilled hole in the bulwark which had been squared with needle files. Small 1/8-in.-by-1/16-in. brass sheaves were inserted into squared drilled holes in the end of the davit and kept in place with a small brass rod as noted in Fig. 40. These davits were inserted through 1/4-in. square receptacle holes which had been drilled and filed square

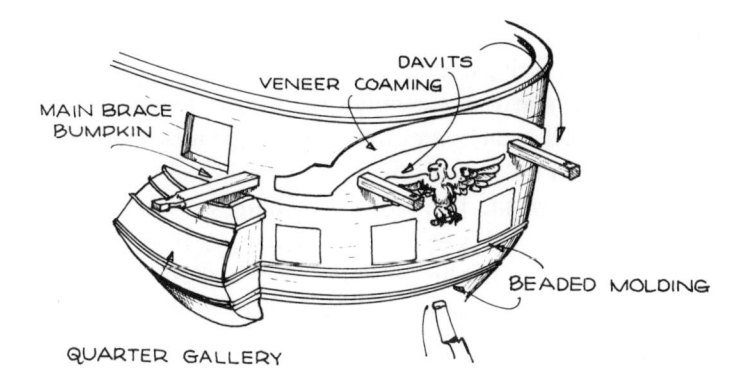

Fig. 38. Stern detail

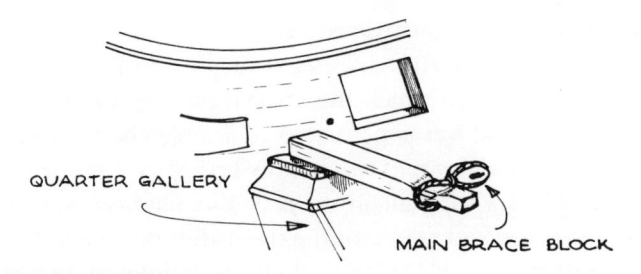

Fig. 39. Main brace bumpkin

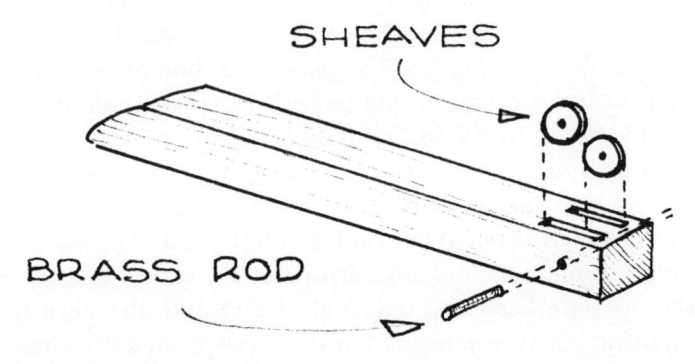

Fig. 40. Stern davits

as noted in the stern bulwark and placed so that approximately 1/2 in. of the davit projected onto the potential spar deck area. These davits were painted flat black.

Inboard Gun Deck Fittings

After completing the stern outboard section, I began work on the inboard gun deck fittings. The captain's stern or transom seat which fitted over the inboard top segment of the rudder (as described in Chapter I, the tiller attachment to the rudder was on the berth deck) was constructed to lie against the stern bulwark below the stern windows as noted in Fig. 41. The morticed cabinet work beneath the seat and the seat top, itself, were constructed of 1/16-in. walnut stock curved and beveled to fit the contours of the transom and innerwale planking. The area immediately forward of the captain's transom seat was left open for approximately 1/2-in. square in order to display the mortice joint with the tiller and the rudder. This was especially important for later attachment of the tiller and its blocks to the steering

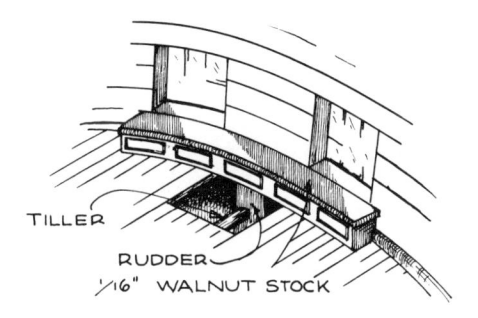

Fig. 41. Transom seat

wheel rope attachment. A captain's trunk was carved from a small piece of walnut, 1/2 in. by 1/2 in. by 3/4 in. long with shim brass utilized for banding held in place with 1/8-in. brass roundhead nails. The lock was fashioned from several eyebolts. The only other items present in the captain's quarters on the model were the captain's bureau and two tables, a chart table and a dining table. These tables were placed below the spar deck skylights to take advantage of sun and moonlight. These three pieces of furniture are as noted in Fig. 42: they were made of small 1/16-in. and 1/8-in. thick pieces of wild cherry. I obtained the wild cherry from a farm near Emmitsburg, Maryland, not far from Baltimore. The standard for excellent furniture was Honduras mahogany although wild cherry was apparently used, especially for table tops; it is very close grained, sands well, and, when varnished, has a beautiful, soft, translucent, red amber color.

Partitions

There were two partitions separating the main gun deck from the captain's quarters, one served as a sort of an atrium or waiting area and the second sectioned off the waiting area from the captain's sleeping quarters. These partitions were constructed of 1/8-in. and 1/32-in. mahogany frames with louvered door frames of 1/16-in.-by-1/8-in. walnut, as shown in Fig. 43. The louvered doors were constructed and morticed as noted and held in place with wire hinges. However, the two that were to be left open permanently in the partition were fixed that way with glue in order to show the entrance between the gun deck and the captain's quarter areas. As previously noted, these partitions on the original vessel were hinged to the spar or main deck beams above so that in times of combat they could be elevated beneath the spar deck or

DINING TABLE   CHART TABLE

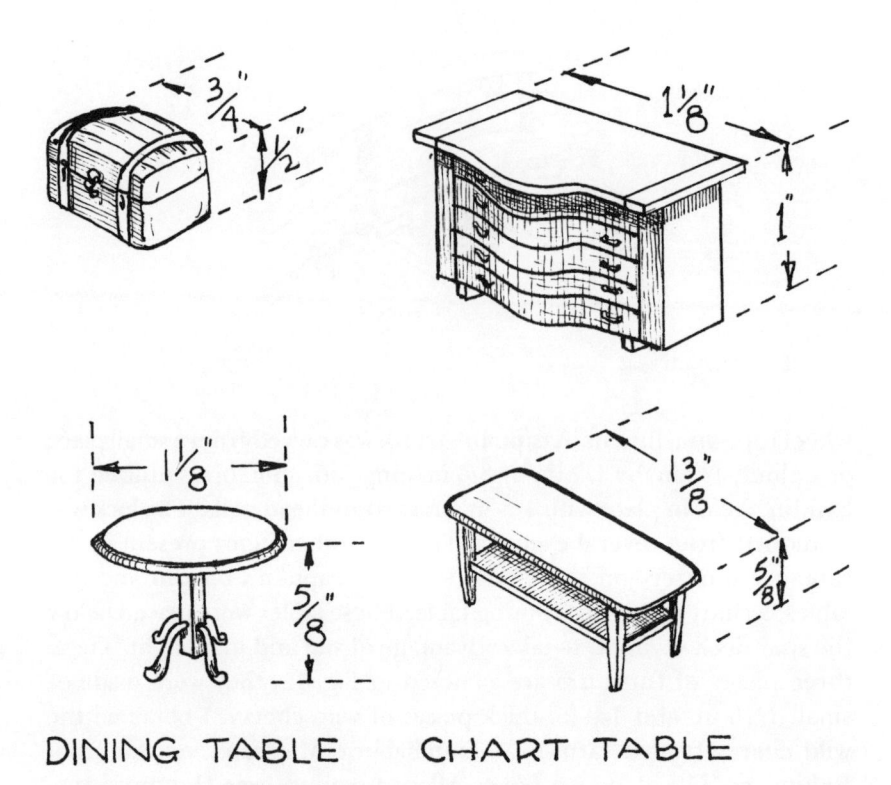

Fig. 42. Captain's furniture

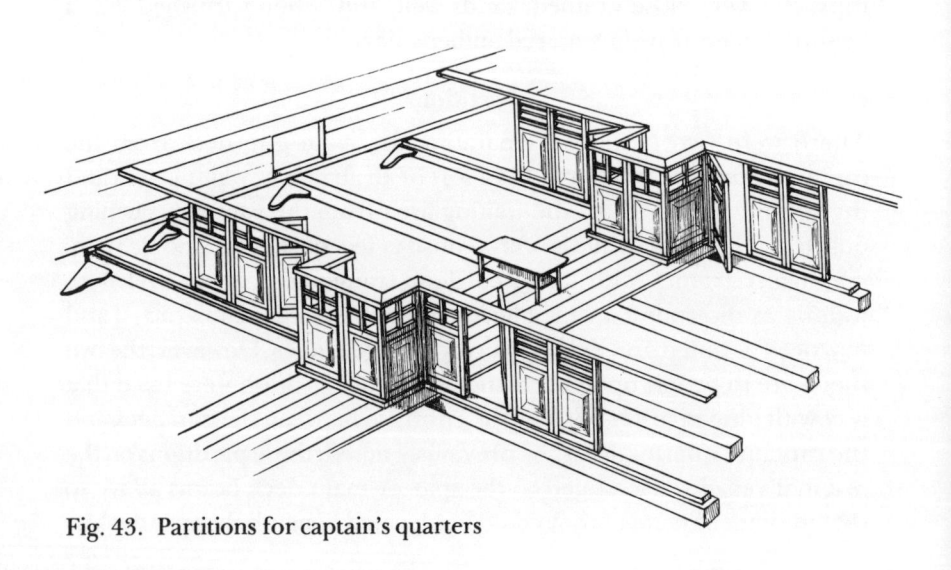

Fig. 43. Partitions for captain's quarters

completely disassembled and taken below the orlop deck to decrease chances of splinter injuries from cannon balls to nearby crew. The partitions were shellacked and given a final coat of spar varnish. The partition height was measured to fit just below the potential location of the beams of the spar deck which were near to being made to size and positioned in place.

Capstans

The capstans were turned from 1/2-in. walnut stock with oak bases. The originals were constructed of laminated oak with iron bandings, particularly at the top so as to give added strength near the capstan bar holes and on the bottom near the iron pawls and ratcheted base. The capstan of the gun deck was attached with 1/8-in. segment of oak dowel to the capstan of the spar deck above so that both capstans could be utilized in unison with two crews when pulling up the anchor. Instead of being made from iron, the banding on the capstan of the model was shim brass painted black, attached with small brass nails with the base banding also made from 1/16-in. brass which had been filed with grooves to simulate the ratchets. The pawls were made from two small pieces of 1/16-in.-by-1-in. filed brass, pinned to the capstan with brass nails thus simulating the winchlike holding mechanism of the capstan. The oakwood base of the capstan and additional features are shown in Fig. 44.

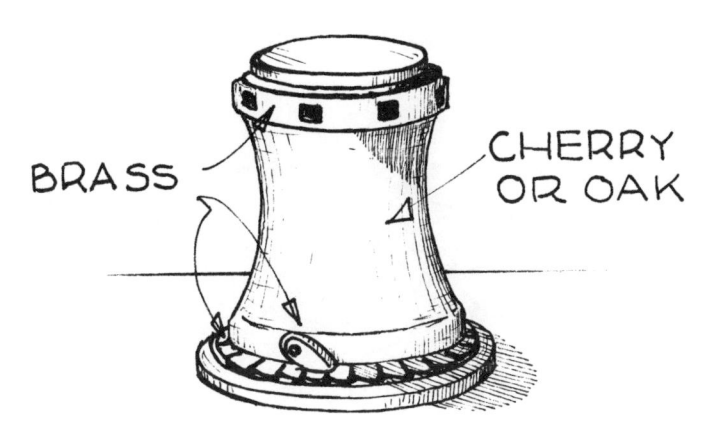

Fig. 44. Capstan

Bilge Pumps

The bilge pumps were constructed as noted in Fig. 45. The coaming border was made of 5/64-in.-by-5/16-in. basswood and the pump cylinders were 3/16-in. dowels which had been drilled with 1/16-in. holes to allow the pump discharging disks to be inserted inside the support pieces. The handle and support disk pieces were made from 1/32-in. brass and .031 wire. The brass was held together utilizing brass nails as rivets as noted in the drawing (Fig. 45). They were clenched together with the small escutcheon pins and mounted on two brass rails which enabled the pumps to teeter-totter manually with pressure similar to the original pump. The crossbar disk pump handles were passed into the drilled dowels. These four dowels passed down though the hatch cover of 1/16-in. basswood to the limber area near the keelson to simulate their position on the original *Constellation*. As noted, the center bars were pivoted to enable the handles to move up and down. The entire apparatus was then covered with two thin coats of shellac prior to assembly.

Cannonball Racks, Etc.

The cannonball racks, ammunition scuttle (shot pots), and chain pots (anchor) were then completed about the multiple hatches as noted in Fig. 46. The cannonball racks were constructed of 1/16-in.-by-1/8-in. basswood with the center section grooved for the placement of the cannonball shot. Number 12 shotgun pellets were utilized to simulate the cannonballs very efficiently. They were epoxied in place to prevent motion. The shot pots were made of small 1/16-in. brass stock drilled and rounded to match its iron shape on the full-sized *Constellation* (Fig. 46).

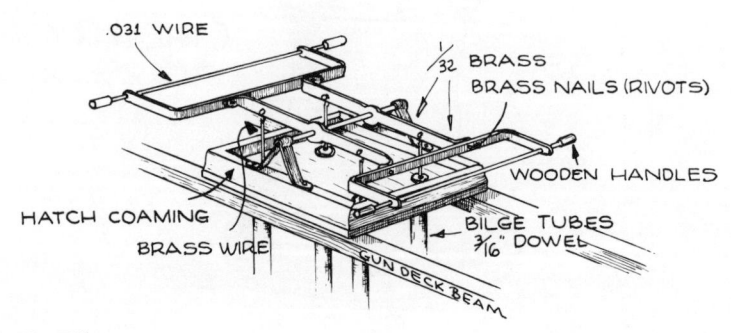

Fig. 45. Bilge pumps

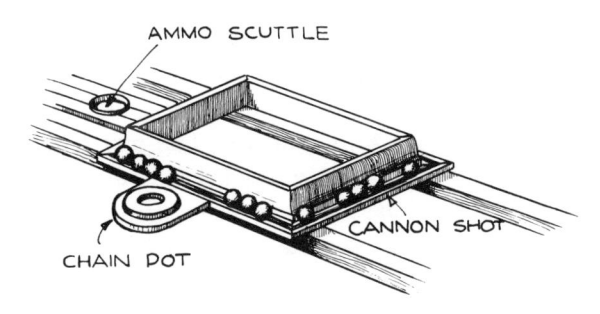

STERN SECTION, QUARTER GALLERIES, FORWARD TIMBERHEADS 55

Fig. 46. Ammo scuttle and shot racks

The Galley

The galley was constructed from small pieces of plank stock, 3/32-in.-by-1/4-in. basswood. The metal front section of the galley was finished with four small ovens and a midsection fireplace all of which were painted black. Pin heads and brass nailheads were used to simulate the handles for these ovens. The top was painted a buff, flat brown color to simulate the original dusty galley roof. The brick was finally adequately simulated out of painted wood after many attempts with other materials. Because I operated on the exacting premise of trying to duplicate materials from the original, I attempted intitially to chip small pieces of red brick 1/16 in. by 1/8 in. by 3/32 in.—this method frankly did not work satisfactorily. I then tried various paint schemes until I struck upon one which duplicates true brick and mortar appearance. After the sides were constructed of wood as indicated in Fig. 47 and before the wooden simulated fireplace and other details were added,

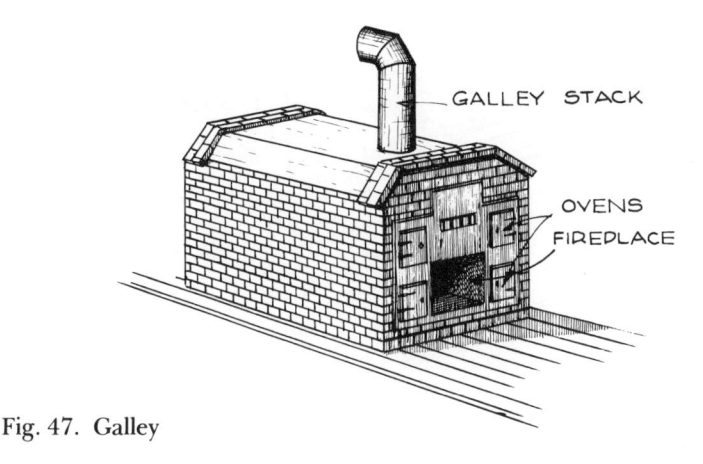

Fig. 47. Galley

the sides were scored with a burrin or awl so that the bricks were 1/16 in. high by 1/8 in. long. After these scored lines were completed both horizontally and perpendicularly, the entire galley was painted flat white to seal the porous wood surface. The entire galley was then painted a dusky red to simulate galley brick. After the red paint had dried thoroughly, the entire galley was again painted flat white (shellac base) making sure that the scored or grooved lines were completely filled with paint. This final surface layer was then wiped off lightly leaving a slightly streaked red brick surface and white mortar simulated in the grooves between the bricks. This method worked very effectively especially in giving a weathered appearance to the streaked red brick which mimicked the salty and blemished "seaside" or "weatherside" look of red brick. After completing the painting, I glued the fireplace section in place. The galley funnel was constructed of 3/8-in. birch dowel, painted flat black, and glued in place (Fig. 47). The entire completed galley was then glued in place on the gun deck.

Anchor Riding Bitts

The oaken rounded anchor riding bitts forward of the galley and the larger square anchor riding bitts aft of the galley were fashioned from 3/8-in. oak stock and glued in place as noted in Fig. 48. The aft riding bitt crossbar was constructed of 1/4-in. square oak wood. The fore riding bitts were 2-3/4 in. high with 3/4 in. rising above the gun deck. The aft riding bitts had an identical height. The support knees on each

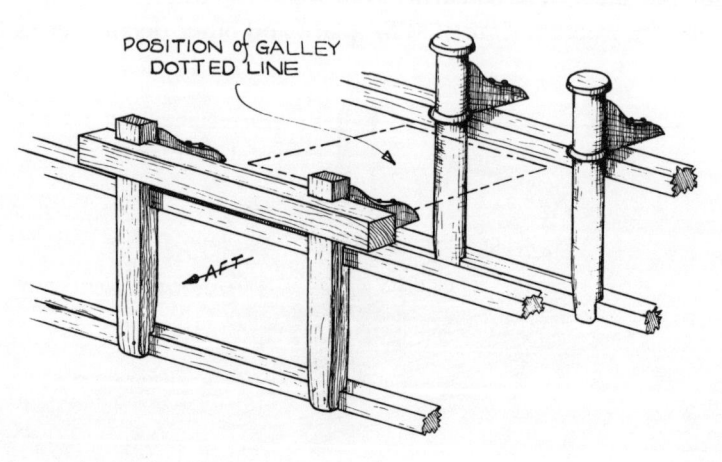

Fig. 48. Anchor riding bitts

STERN SECTION, QUARTER GALLERIES, FORWARD TIMBERHEADS 57

set of bitts were constructed of 1/8-in. oak with brass nails to simulate the large bronze or iron bolts used on the full-size *Constellation*.

Gun Carriages

The only other major structure of the gun deck other than the bowsprit bitts (or support timbers) are the multiple gun carriages which were installed before work was commenced on the spar deck beams because it would be extremely difficult to fix the gun carriages in place and rig their tackles while working through and between the spar deck beams.

Construction of the gun carriages for the 18-pound naval truck guns was relatively simple. I adopted the plans from those of Mr. Leon Polland (1974), which were obtained from English prototypes and the USF *Constitution*. Fig. 49 illustrates the size and dimension of the carriage; Fig. 50 illustrates the method by which the trucks (wheels) were made for the gun carriages; Fig. 51 illustrates the dimensions of the cannon and its construction; Fig. 52 demonstrates the positioning of the cannon carriage at the gunport with appropriate gun tackle purchases. The dimensions with respect to carriage and gun are as noted in those respective figures. The cheeks were constructed from 1/8-in. oak stock, shaped to the dimensions necessary, specifically 5/8

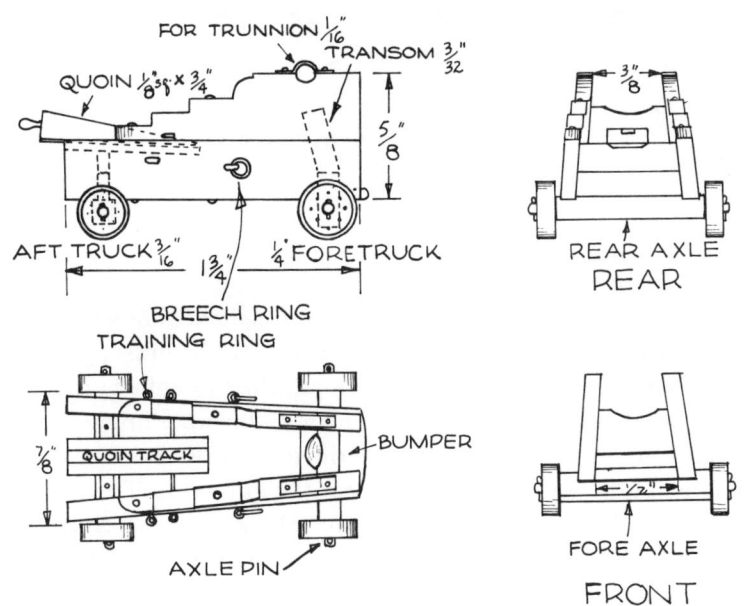

Fig. 49. Eighteen-pound gun carriage

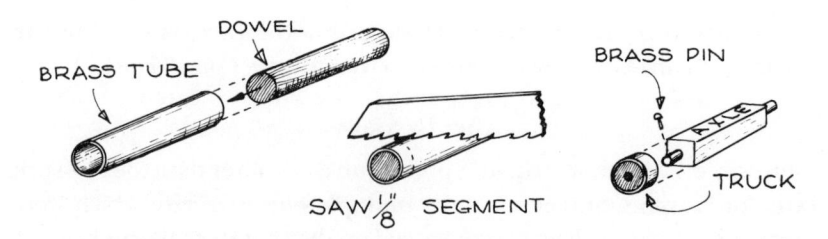

Fig. 50. Truck construction

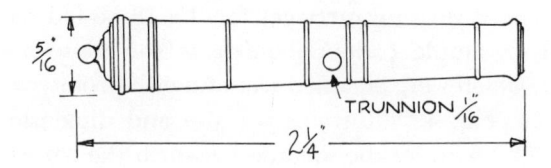

Fig. 51. Eighteen-pound naval gun

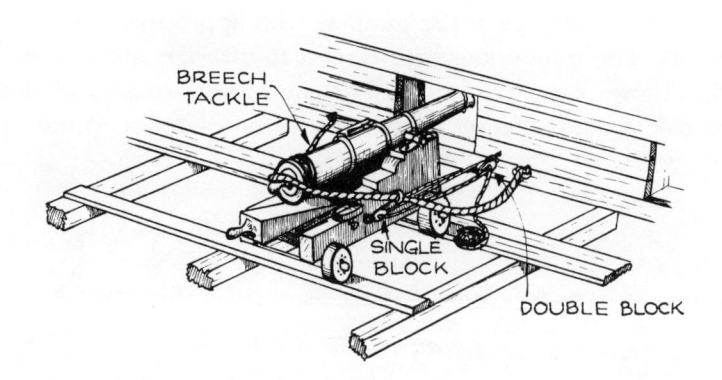

Fig. 52. Breech and training tackles

in. high and 1-3/8 in. long. The grooves for the trunnions were filed with 1/16-in. needle file to adequately fit the 1/16-in. brass trunnions of the cannon. Two small eyebolts were attached to either side of each cheek, one serving as a breeching ring and the other one serving as a training ring to which was mounted the gun tackles prior to its subsequent attachment to the bulwarks near the gun ports. The axles were made from 1/8-in.-by-1/8-in. basswood, the ends of which had been carved circumferentially to 1/16 in. to receive the trucks. The transom for the carriage was fashioned from 1/8-in. basswood and glued in place between the cheeks which stabilized them. Small brass roundhead nails were utilized on the top of the steplike cuts of each cheek to simulate the through and through bolts which are utilized on the full-size carriages to hold together the plank pieces making up each one of the cheeks. Obviously, this is not necessary on the model. After completion of cheeks and axles, various methods were attempted to make the fore and aft trucks. I initially attempted to wrap sections of rounded wood or dowel with brass wrappings cut from pieces of shim brass and attached them with brass nails; however, the trucks split easily and this method was not reliable. I then used 1/4-in. brass tube for the fore trucks and 3/16-in. brass tube for the aft trucks into which I inserted or incarcerated a piece of preshaped dowel, similar in dimensions to the inside diameter of both the 1/4-in. and 3/16-in. hollow brass tube. These were cut off at 1/8-in. intervals as noted in Fig. 50 thus making strapped wheels or trucks similar to the carriage wheels on the original vessel and to the wheels of Victorian carriages, buckboards, etc. After completion of each one of these trucks, a 1/16-in. hole was drilled in the center to adequately fit the 1/16-in. rounded axle. After the trucks were placed on the axles, small holes were drilled transversely though the axles at the junction of the trucks, and small, molded, modelmaker's nails were inserted through these holes, bent slightly, the pointed ends cut off to simulate the large Carter keys of the full-sized gun carriages. After completion of the axles, transom, and trucks, the quoin was made from 1/8-in. oak stock. A dowel 1/16 in., rounded and tapered to form a handle shape, was inserted into the back of each quoin to serve as a handle or purchase with which to pull the quoin out or push it forward. The quoin moved on a small track which was constructed from 1/16-in.-by-1/16-in. oak strip which was then glued onto the aft axle. In this way, the quoin could move in and out which either elevated or depressed the breech of the cannon for aiming purposes at the time of the cannon firing. The quoin is referred to in the English literature as a wedge.

Cannons

After completion of the carriage, the cannon proper were made with dimensions and sizes as noted in Fig. 51. The initial cannons were constructed from 3/8-in. brass rod which was turned on a shopsmith. Since I did not have a metal lathe available, I used a standard, 3/8-in. drill chuck into which I inserted a brass rod. The other end of the brass rod was inserted into a hole in a fixed piece of oak at the end of a shopsmith which had a 3/8-in. hole drilled in it to receive the opposite end of the brass rod. This obviously had to be centered coincidently or concentrically with the chuck level. Because of the large number of 18-pound cannons needed (24 on the gun deck and 2 on the spar deck), it became obvious that painstakingly turning each cannon would be a prolonged process and it would save time if the cannons were cast. I therefore obtained some jeweler's casting rubber and made several molds very simply by suspending the cannon in glass and pouring the molten rubber around the cannon. After the rubber had dried, it was incised in a uniform, transverse fashion in the midline of the cannon, thus making an identical two-piece mold. The mold was squared prior to this cutting to make sure that the edges were equal and that it would fit together readily. This mold was used to cast most of the cannons with the exception of the two spar deck cannons which were turned on a lathe. These were cast in lead although I also tried plastic. There was no particular reason, I felt to be turning them out of brass in attempts to simulate the originals when, in fact, the originals were not made out of brass at all but out of cast iron or bronze. After completion of the cannon including drilling of the muzzle, approximately 1/4-in. deep with a 1/64-in. drill, the cannons were mounted on the small carriages or cheeks with 1/16-in. brass shim strips which had been molded to fit over the trunnions and onto the cheeks. Small holes were drilled on both sides of the trunnions into which were inserted roundheaded brass nails to fix the trunnions to the cheeks.

Gun Tackles

After completion of the carriages, they were attached to the bulwarks of the gun deck in the usual way. The breeching tackle was made from 1/16-in. rolling twine which, as it is woven and twisted, readily simulates the old-time hemp or Manila rope which was used for breech rope. It was attached to bulwark eyebolts on each side of the gunport. The aiming tackle was made in the following way: a single block was stropped and served to the eyebolt of the cheek. A standing purchase was then made through the loop strop of the single block and then rove through a double block which was stropped or fixed to an eyebolt on one side of the gunport. The rope was then rove through the single cheek block, back through the double block, and then placed on the deck in a small coil in a ship-shape manner, "ready for action," so to speak. Several of the cannons were not put through the gunports at various levels for variation to demonstrate the full-sized cannon gun with carriages; the breech tackle was also disconnected from the eyebolt purchase near the bulwark so that area could be visualized. An example of a completed gun carriage with cannon and gun tackles in place on the bulwark is shown in Fig. 52. In order to not block a view of the berth deck below, the gun carriages were mounted on small, incomplete pieces of planking, 1/16 in. thick and 1/8 in. wide in short lengths, attached just underneath the carriages or close to those areas where the gun carriage trucks would be near the supporting frames, as noted in Fig. 53.

Spar Deck

The spardeck was constructed in a similar fashion to the previous decks and was parallel to the plank sheer and outboard planking, approximately 1-5/8 in. from the top of the gun deck beams to the top of the spar deck beams. The previously employed deck placement jig (Fig.14) was used to mark the level of the spar deck waterway and the length of the beam (Fig.15) was premeasured in a similar fashion to the other deck beams from frame to frame. They were cut from 1/4-in. square, slightly cambered oak, sanded, glued, and nailed in place with appropriate thrust knees (as noted in Plate III) to each beam. After completion of the spar deck, waterways were placed about the entire periphery of this deck at the junction of the spar deck beams with the bulwarks. This waterway was constructed of 3/32-in.-by-1/4-in. beech which had been lightly steam heated to facilitate its bending. As noted, beechwood is extremely malleable and readily bent to conform to the compound contours of the bow and stern.

Gangways

The gangways between the fore and aft sections of the spar deck were constructed as shown (Fig. 53). There was approximately one step down or approximately a foot between the fore and aft sections of the spar deck to the gangway. On the model, the gangways were constructed of 1/16-in.-by-1/8-in. basswood planks as noted, attached to the low level of the waterway, approximately 1/8 in. below the level of what would be the planking height of the spar decks. Eight ladders were constructed similarly to the ladders (hatch ladders) between the berth and gun decks. These also utilized 1/8-in.-by-1/16-in. basswood frames (styles) in which 1/32-in. grooves had been cut out to

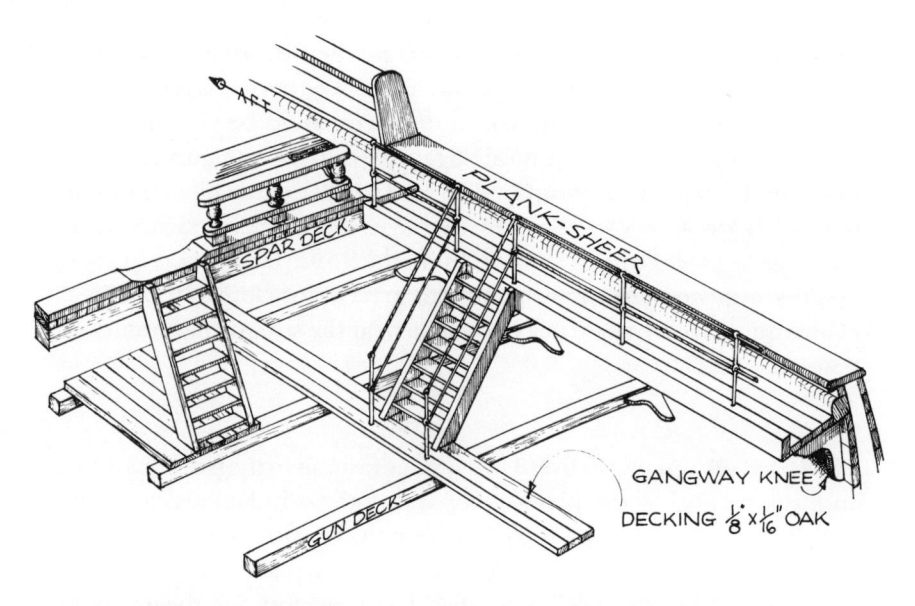

Fig. 53. Gangway, ladders, and railing

receive the rungs (treads) of 1/32-in.-by-1/8-in. shim basswood. The overall size of the ladders was 5/8 in. by 2-1/2 in. approximately. There were four ladders at each aft and fore section of the spar deck: two from the gangways to the gun deck and two from the aft and fore spar deck to the gun deck (Fig. 53). Fig. 53 shows the railings athwartships at the junction of the spar deck, fore and aft, with the open gun deck. These were made of cherry stock, 1/4-in. square for the stanchions and 1/4 in. by 1/16 in. for the cherry wood curved-edge railing (Fig. 53). The railings between the stanchions beautifully demonstrate the characteristics of this kind of wild cherry wood. When quarter sawed, the transverse radiations (right angles to the annual rings) are clearly, naturally highlighted especially after being varnished or shellacked. The transverse radiations are similar to those one might see on old. fumed oak and fiddleback maple antique furniture pieces. The double-roped railing stanchions of each of the companionways (Fig. 53) were 3/4-in. high, circular brass, with 1/64-in. holes drilled at the upper and midsection of the stanchions to hold the rope railings. I initially placed these rope railings inboard but would advise anyone constructing the model to leave the ropes off until much later in the construction of the model because when constructing the other fittings for the spar

STERN SECTION, QUARTER GALLERIES, FORWARD TIMBERHEADS 63

deck and vessel rigging, these railings and stanchions get caught in tools and fittings repeatedly requiring them to be tightened to maintain a ship-shape appearance. The athwartship wooden railings were mounted on two layers of 3/32-in.-by-1-in. planking to match the plank height of the spar deck and give support to the railing as noted in Fig. 54.

Bitts and Fife Rails

There were two sets of bitts, immediately forward of the fore spar deck athwartship railing and were constructed of 1/4-in. square cherry stock with transverse dowels and 1/16-in. maple. They were mounted to the gun deck and spar deck beams as noted in Fig. 55. An identical set, port and starboard, were mounted lateral to the capstan of the aft spar deck and glued and nailed to the spar and gun deck beams.

Four additional ladders were again constructed identical to the previous ladders between the berth and orlop decks and were placed in the hatch entrances between the aft spar deck and the gun deck in a similar fashion to those illustrated.

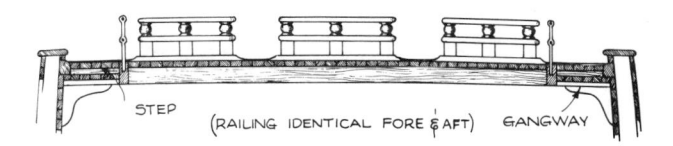

Fig. 54. Spar deck railings

Fig. 55. Bitts (port and starboard)

The mizzenmast bitts were constructed of cherry wood, 1/4 in. square by 2-3/4 in. long, with transverse cross members of 1/16-in. maple dowel. They were anchored to the gun deck and spar deck frames as noted in Fig. 56. Small brass cleats were mounted and inserted on each side of the bitt timbers for yard sling purchase.

The mainmast bitts and fife rails are as indicated in Fig. 57. The bitts which are forward of the mast are similar in size to the mizzenmast bitts or 1/4-in. square cherry wood with small brass cleats also on each side of the bitt timbers.

The fife rail stanchions were morticed to the deck beams with the upper portion turned on the lathe to the configuration shown (Fig. 57). The stanchions were made of 5/16-in. cherry wood stock; the base of

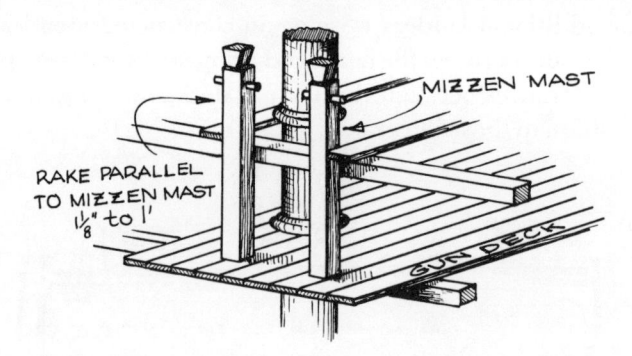

Fig. 56. Mizzen bitts

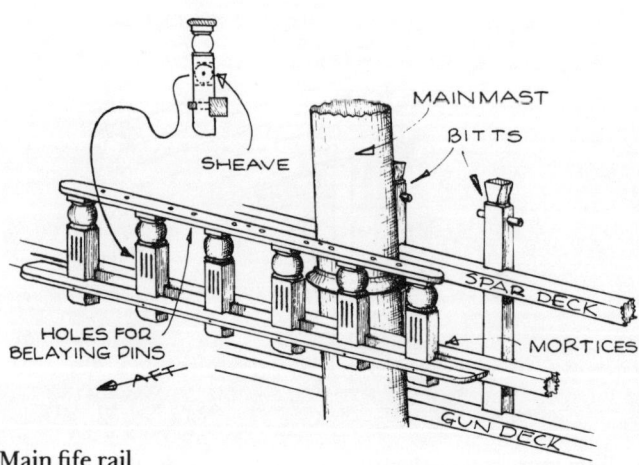

Fig. 57. Main fife rail

each having triple sheaves which were inserted into rectangular holes in the bottom through which would eventually be rove the yard lifts. These sheaves were 1/8-in. brass rod stock which had been cut 1/32-in. thick, filed smooth and drilled centrally to permit passage of a .031-in. brass rod to hold the sheaves in place in the stanchion. There are several methods by which the slots in the timbers and stanchions may be cut out for the sheave. One method is to drill multiple 1/32-in. holes in a small, linear, longitudinal line along the stanchion square piece and then chisel out the intervening material. The method I employed was to drill the top and bottom of the rectangular area involved and then take a small, 3/16-in. modelmaker's chisel and incise the lines and literally carve out the area into which the sheave was to be inserted. The small, rectangular hole could then be filed with square needle files to square off each corner. After the slots were cut to size, smoothed and sanded, the brass rod cut sheaves were inserted in place and held in place with the brass rod. The top rail of the fife rail was constructed of 1/4-in.-by-1/16-in. cherry wood with the edges gently rounded before nailing and gluing in position on the already secured fife rail stanchions. The top of the fife rail was drilled with 1/32-in. diameter holes at appropriate intervals for insertion of the belaying pins (as noted in the belaying pin plan on Plate III.) The morticed segment at the bottom part of the stanchions was made from a piece of deck planking, 1/8 in. by 1/16 in., and glued into the mortice with epoxy. All sections of the bitts, stanchions, and fife rail were then glued in place on the spar and gun decks. The fore bitts and associated fife rail near the foremast were constructed in an identical fashion to the mainmast fife rail with the exception that the fife rail was attached by two linear belaying pin racks to the fore bitt heads or timberheads. This created a standing belaying pin rack on each side of the foremast for additional locations to mount bowsprit and foremast yard rigging. The only additional difference between the main fife rail and the foremast fife rail is that there were six stanchions with the mainmast fife rail and only five with the foremast fife rail. The fife railing was also constructed as were the intervening belaying pin racks of 1/4-in.-by-1./6-in. rounded edge cherry. The top rail of the fife rail was morticed into the belaying pin rack running forward to the bitts, appropriately shaped, glued, and then drilled with multiple 1/32-in. drill holes for the belaying pins as illustrated in Fig. 58. The foremast bitts were attached to the cross deck beams of the spar and gun deck prior to gluing and nailing of the

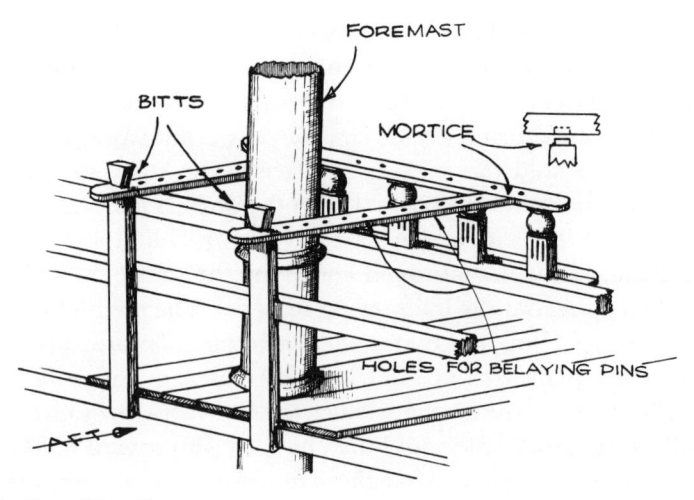

Fig. 58. Fore fife rail

belaying pin rack. The belaying pin rack was notched out to fit the tapered timberheads of the fore bitts prior to gluing.

Except for discussing the construction of the skylights, steering wheel, and binnacle, I have been proceeding in a kind of aft-forward direction and after several brief comments on the construction of the bowsprit support timber or bitts between gun deck and spar deck, I will advance to the construction of the bow timberheads, stempiece, and seat and head rail construction of the bow.

Small Fittings

Between the gun deck and spar deck, approximately 3 in. from the bow stempiece, two bowsprit support pieces or bitts were constructed of 1/4-in. oak morticed to the gun deck below and the spar deck above which were glued and bolted in place to receive the squared end of the octagonal-shaped and trimmed bowsprit butt. Immediately prior to this construction, a 5/8-in. hole had been drilled in the centerline bow bulwark and taper filed to receive the end of the bowsprit. The bottom of this hole coincided with the tapered end of the stempiece so that the bowsprit could be later gammoned to the stem piece with hemp rope. These two beams or bowsprit bitts, which support the inner butt of the bowsprit, are shown in Fig. 59.

The only other minor gun deck fittings which have not been discussed are the small anchor pawls or "pinch cleats" on both sides of

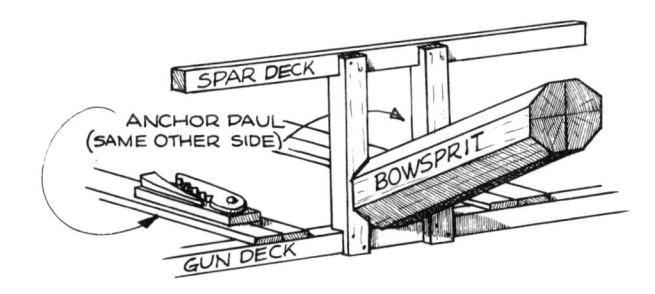

STERN SECTION, QUARTER GALLERIES, FORWARD TIMBERHEADS   67

Fig. 59. Bowsprit supports

the bowsprit bitts. These are small parts fashioned of 1/8-in.-by-1/4-in. basswood stock with a pin inserted for a pivot with several small carved indentions and mounted on a 1/4-in.-by-1/16-in.-by-1/2-in. piece of oak to represent the notched or ratcheted grooves which act as stopper cleats or teeth for the anchor hawser (Fig. 59).

Bow and Stem Pieces

We now come to one of the most difficult yet most interesting parts of the model ship and, in some ways, the most intriguing and beautiful to envision on any ship or its model of this vintage: specifically, the bow and the carved stempieces with related structures. First of all, it is necessary to have the bow bulwark and timberhead sections completed before adding the stempieces, head rail, and head-knee construction as these parts attach to the bow bulwark. Fig. 60 demonstrates the construction of the bow bulwark and timberheads. The plank sheer forward of the second gunport or end plank of the forward bulwark was approximately a foot above the deck on the real vessel or 1/4 in. above

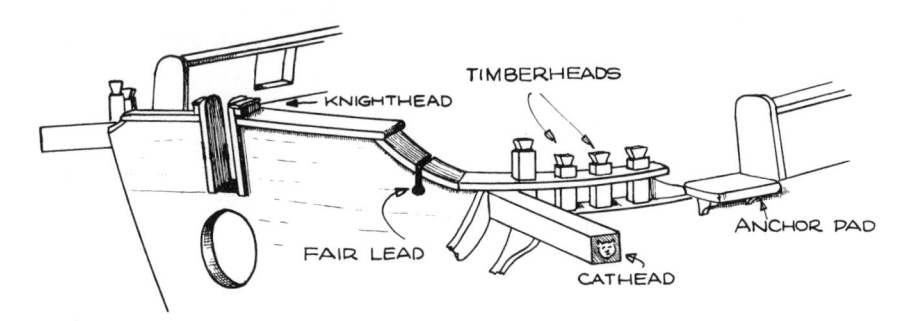

Fig. 60. Bow timberheads

the spar deck waterway on the model. After the spar deck had been constructed, the spar deck waterway, made of 3/32-in.-by-1/4-in. beechwood, was nailed in place, coinciding to the shape of the bow bulwark as outlined in Fig. 61.

Instead of trying to carve or reshape the timberheads of each canted frame forward to coincide and be morticed with the kennel rail, most of the constructed fore frames were cut down to the plank sheer line as noted except the most forward frame near the knighthead which was cut essentially as shown (Fig. 61). The small side gangway end planks of the bowsprit walkway, mounted next to the knighthead, were made of 1/16-in.-by-5/8-in.-by-1-1/4-in. cherry wood with the edges round and tapered before gluing in place and after the bulwarks had been painted flat white inside and flat black outside. The bow bulwarks were approximately 1-1/4 in. high above the bow spar deck waterway for approximately 2 in. laterally before they began their slow taper to the lower plank-sheer level or to the level of approximately the second gunport opening. The plank-sheer rails were fashioned from 1/16-in. thick oak strips which had been carved to meet the bow curvature and then glued in place. The plank-sheer at this level was flush with the side planking of the hull (black) before beginning its upward curve at the fore side of the cathead.

After completion of the main topside shape of the bow bulwark, the catheads were constructed of 3/8-in. oak stock and glued and nailed in place. On the original vessel, a cat beam was secured underneath the cathead to act as a carling beam strengthener to better secure the cathead to the frames. As the deck is open on this particular model, the catheads are shown with their flush attachment to the spar deck beams without intervening planks. The size and shape of the cathead are as noted in Fig. 62. A small cat's face, 1/16 in. by 1/4 in. by 1/4 in., was carved of wild cherry stock and glued on the fore end of the cathead

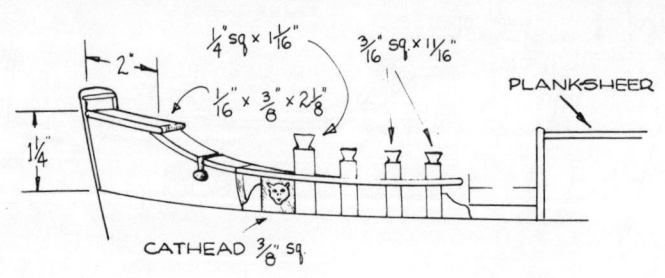

Fig. 61. Bow dimensions

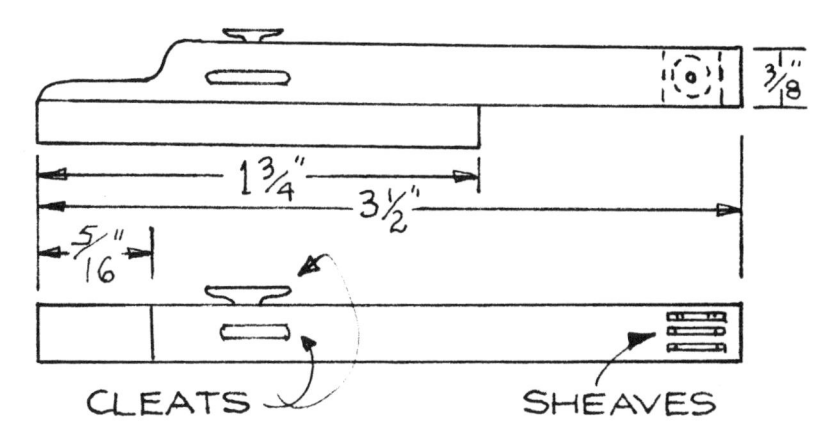

Fig. 62. Cathead

after being painted gold. Three sheaves, 3/16 in. by 1/16 in., were constructed from brass rod in an identical fashion to the sheave construction of the fife rails and held in place in the end of the cathead in the rectangular carved holes by brass wire of approximately .04 in. in diameter. The holes for insertion of the sheaves were again constructed similar to those of the fife rails stanchions which were drilled, chiseled square, and then filed smoothly to accept the inserted grooved brass sheaves.

After the catheads had been constructed, glued, and nailed in position, the framing of the curved bulwark was completed inboard and outboard with 3/32-in.-by-1/4-in. basswood planking to coincide with the outside hull planking and the end pieces were then cut off or carved in the curvilinear fashion to match the curved shape of the bow bulwark. The kennel frame and fore timberheads on each side, starboard and port, were made from walnut stock. Two main timberheads of the head rails were cut from 1/4-in.-by-1/4-in.-by-1/2-in. walnut with squared, morticed timberheads. The other timberheads, six in number, were cut from 3/16-in. stock, and all of the timberheads were cut square and indented in a similar fashion to the mast bitts. The kennel railing was carved from 1/16-in. walnut sheet (Fig. 61). The base of each timberhead above the plank sheer and under the kennel railing was made from walnut stock, 5/16 in. in height and 1/4 in. or 3/16 in. square for the head rail timberhead and remaining aft timberheads respectively. Two small walnut curved knees at the junction of the cathead and most aft timberhead on the plank sheer were then shaped, carved, and glued in place. A small anchor pad was also made from 1/8-in.-by-5/16-in.-by-1-in. oak stock with the edges rounded and curved, and this was glued in place on the plank sheer behind the aft timberhead and close to the fore end of the side bulwark leaving a 1/16-in. space for insertion of the end plank piece similar to the pieces that had been inserted in the side of the bowsprit waterway. Two small knee pieces were fashioned from 1/16-in. oak stock and placed underneath the overhanging anchor pad and coinciding in angle to the tumblehome or angulation of the bow planking as noted in Fig. 63. The anchor pad and small contiguous knees were painted flat black.

After completing the timberheads, I cut out the bow bulwark plank sheer piece from 1/16-in. walnut stock painted white and cut the fairlead into the bowsprit bulwark (Fig. 60). With the timberheads and rails completed, I cut, curved, and beveled to fit the angle of the inboard bow and secured into place with nails and glue the two belaying pin racks of the bow bulwark made of 1/4-in.-by-1/8-in.-by-1-3/4-in. cherry wood. The nails were 3/8-in. thin steel nails with preliminary holes drilled through the cherry wood before hammering them into the bulwark planks and frames. Seven 1/32-in. holes were drilled in each belaying pin rack to receive the 1/2-in. brass belaying pins (7 port and 7 starboard). These holes were drilled parallel to the angle or the anterior tilt of the bow bulwark and not perpendicular to the waterway or spar deck. This way a rope could be more readily purchased and released from the lower part of the belaying pin without pulling against the bulwark. This belaying pin rack is shown in Fig. 64. The belaying pins were turned from 1/16-in. brass rod that had been placed or inserted in a drill chuck on a shopsmith and filed or turned in a similar fashion to several of the 18-pound cannons. Since 1/2-in. brass belaying pins are readily available from ship model fitting stores, I don't think it is necessary to make them and that no one would be criticized

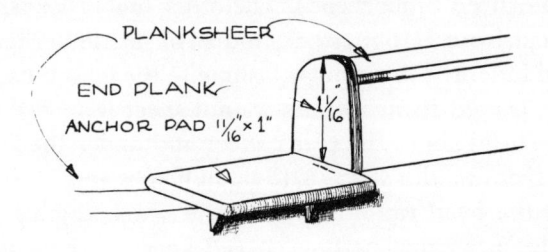

Fig. 63. Anchor pad

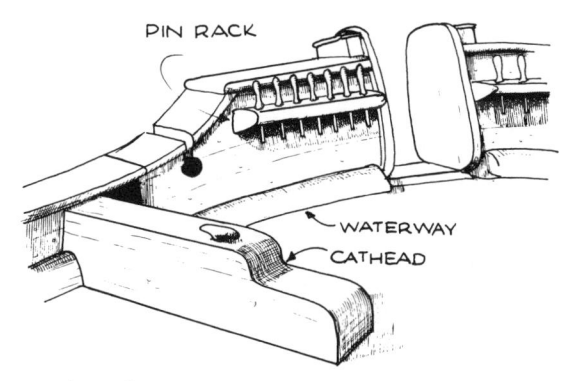

Fig. 64. Bow pin rack

for lack of historical model authenticity by purchasing them. The belaying pins of the remainder of the ship's pin racks and those of the fife rails were also of 1/16-in.-by-1/2-in. brass construction. On the original vessel, these belaying pins were of solid white oak or bronze, but unless they were made of bronze, they had a high mortality rate and required replacement repeatedly.

Carving the Stempiece and Billet Head

We now come to the most challenging part of the bow construction, the carved sides of the stempieces and billet head. A side view of the stem piece and curlicues or scroll work are as noted in Fig. 65. The two moldings above and below the stempiece scroll work are called upper and lower trail cheeks. They were doubly grooved, or beaded molding, carved from 1/4-in.-by-1/8-in. pieces of beech wood. Although this wood is hollow grained and is carved with some difficulty because of its compressibility, it serves well for making these curved cheeks because of this very quality as they need to be curved to the shape of the stempiece and tapered progressively to a narrower width near the billet head. The two moldings were shaped, sanded, and cut somewhat oversize in length and not glued in place until the scroll work had been completed on the stempiece. The scroll work could be carved out of a solid piece of the stem after the attachment to the hull, but I would not recommend this difficult route. Having done some walnut and oak carving for baroque furniture, I can say without hesitation that there is marked difficulty in carving small, thin delicate scroll or acanthus leaf type patterns in base relief which are under 1/16 in. in thickness. After several unsatisfactory attempts at relief carving the stem, I came upon

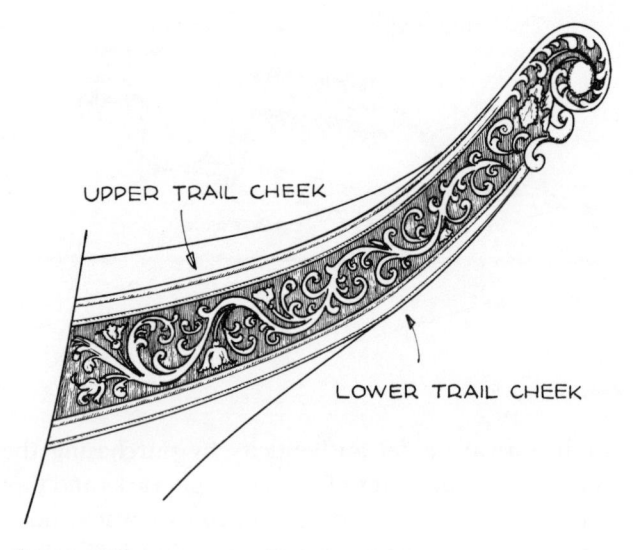

Fig. 65. Stem scroll

the following method which proves very facile and relatively simple. I fashioned a sheet of 1/16-in. oak to match the shape of the curved stempiece and marked off with pencil the top and bottom lines where the upper and lower trail cheeks should be glued in place. After these were marked, I traced the shape of the scroll curves onto this oak piece, and, with a 5 cc. disposable syringe (which may be purchased inexpensively or obtained from your local medical practitioner) filled with vinyl plaster coating or oak sawdust mixed with epoxy glue, I injected on top of this small oak shim the general pattern of the scroll design and shape to coincide to the shape of the scroll. The syringe method cuts down tremendously on the amount of inlay material needed to be carved, the scroll is sturdier, and the scroll pattern can be "tightened up" and perfected in size and shape with small carving knives. This base oak piece with the superimposed scroll pattern can then be painted with the scroll white and the background flat black and can be glued in place on the vessel's stempiece as noted in Fig. 66. The beaded or tapered and molded upper and lower trail cheeks can then be nailed with 1/4-in. small roundheaded brass nails to the stempiece and may be easily painted before or after installation.

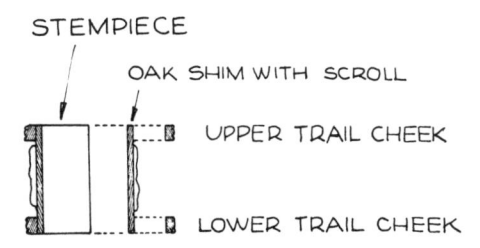

Fig. 66. Cross section stem

Hawseholes

The hawseholes and planking were constructed next, the details as noted in Fig. 67. A double layer of 3/16-in.-by-1/4-in. planking was placed over the initial hull plank layer to coincide with the line contiguous with the outer border of the upper and lower trail cheeks reflected onto the hull. The hawseholes, two each, port and starboard, were then drilled with a 3/16-in. twist drill at approximately a 45° angle to enter the gun deck at the upper border of the gun deck waterway. The tapered or angled hawsehole covers were then fashioned from boxwood, 5/8 in. by 1/2 in., and glued in place. The upper and lower trail cheeks were then constructed as a reflection on the hull from the stempiece down over the hull above and below the hawseholes as noted in the illustration.

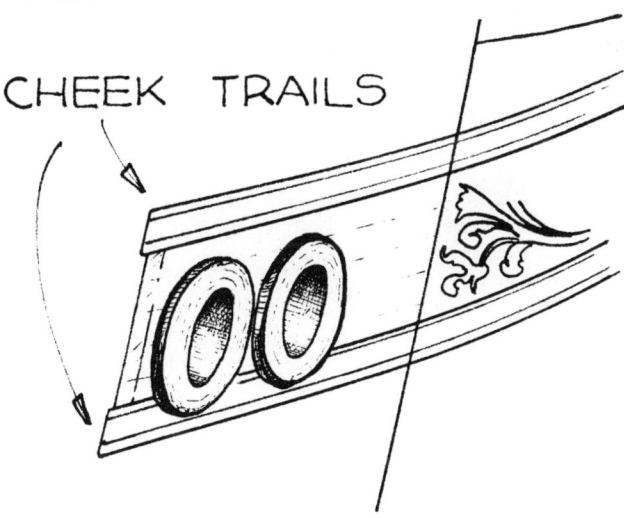

Fig. 67. Hawseholes

After completion of the hawseholes, work may then be initiated on head knees and head rails. Top and side views of the head rails and knees are shown in Fig. 68(A) and (B). End views of the head knees are illustrated in Fig. 69. A completed pen-and-ink sketch of the stempiece, head knees, and rails is noted in Fig. 70. The seat and head rails were fashioned from 1/8-in. oak stock. It should be noted parenthetically that the head and seat rails were constructed to serve as the "outhouse bench" for the regular ablebodied seamen who were forced to brave the elements when nature called. (This area began to be known as the head, and, obviously, this naval expression has persisted.) The upward curve of the rails may be readily determined from Plates I through IV. However, its true shape and fit from the pinnacle of the billet head to the side of the hull must be determined by trial and error

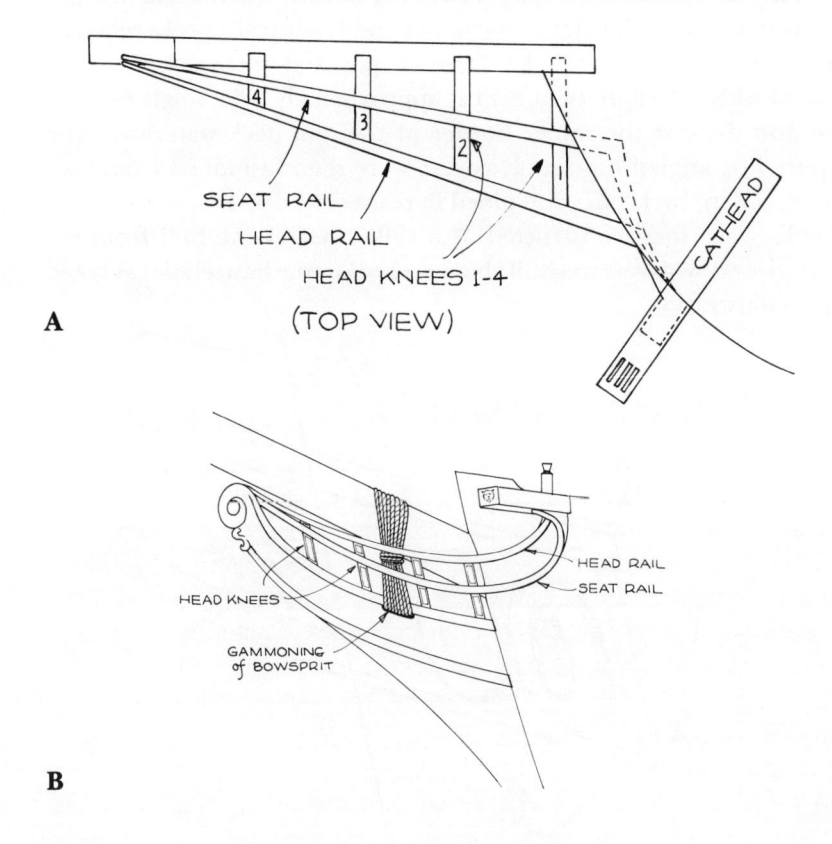

Fig. 68. Head rails, top view, (A), and side view, (B)

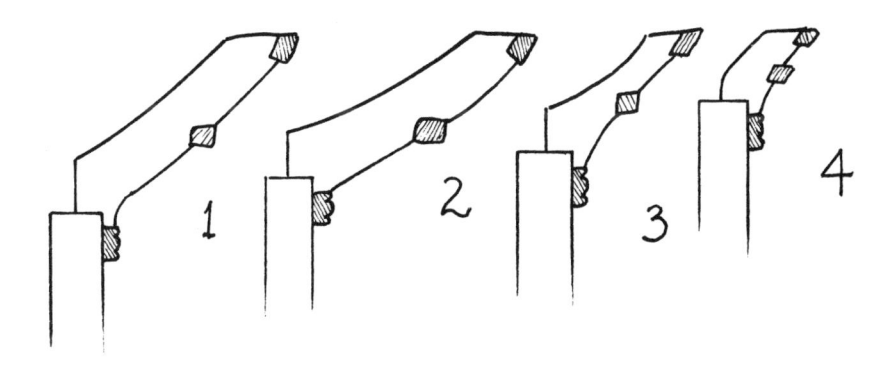

Fig. 69. Head knees

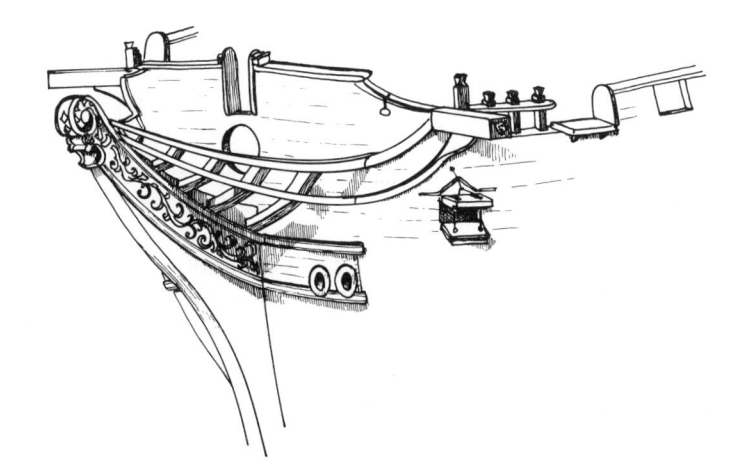

Fig. 70. Head rail and knees

because with a tapered thin plate of wood, it is difficult to represent pictorially all three dimensions and because any variation of contour along the way significantly alters the shape and fit of these head rails. Their measurements must be made from the stempiece and hull once the stempiece and hull have been constructed. I suggest you not worry about how many pieces of good white oak are perhaps wasted in an attempt to determine the true shape of the head and seat rails. At any rate, once the rails have been constructed, they may be glued and nailed in position. The head knees, constructed from 3/16-in. basswood and oak, the end views of which are noted (Fig. 69), were notched and glued in place after their construction after they were angled to match the anterior angle or rake of the stempiece. Some modelmaker's would prefer to mount the knees first and then construct and attach the head and seat rails. That method did not appeal to me as it is difficult to judge the size of the knees and to hold their position without the rails in place, whereas if the head rails are in place, they may be shaped with repeated measurements until they satisfactorily fit between the stem and the rails. Regardless of method, the construction of this portion of the ship is somewhat tedious, however, once completed it can be extremely attractive. By repeated trial and error methods, by tapering and cutting the angle of the head knees with periodic measurements, I obtained nicely fitted, sloped head knees which were then attached and glued in place. The continuation of each head and seat rail onto the hull, going up to the cathead, was then constructed of 3/32-in.-by-1/4-in. beech wood and nailed in place. When superimposed or attached onto the hull, these railings are called ekeings. The upper head rail ekeing terminates in a timberhead in front of the position of the cathead and the seat rail terminates in a "hanging knee" type structure attached to the bottom surface of the cathead, nailed and glued in place. The details of the ekeings are also as noted (Fig. 65). Head rails and knees were then painted flat white and a small white bolster, 1/16 in. by 1/16 in.-by-1/2 in., was fitted on the upper side of the gammoning hole in the stem to cut down functionally on rope chaff after the bowsprit had been attached with the large gammoning ropes (Fig. 66). Details of the placement of the bowsprit gammoning will be discussed below.

Anchors

The anchors were constructed as noted in Fig. 71(A). The anchor bases with flukes may be lead cast, filed brass, or wood painted black. The stock of the anchor was 2-1/2-in.-long-by-1/4-in. square oak, the transverse bands fashioned from shim brass, 3/32 in. wide and held in place with small brass or flat head nails, drilled through the brass and into the wood prior to insertion. These brass bands were painted black to simulate the iron bands on the oak stock of the original vessel. The anchors were then mounted or secured to several eyebolts drilled into several of the gun deck frames immediately aft of the anchor pawls near the bowsprit bitts. The anchors were placed so that one of the flukes rested on the oak pad aft of the exposed bow timberheads: its anchor chain (nine links to the inch) passed through the aft hawsehole and then was secured onto the ring eyebolt of the gun deck beam.

Ordinarily, this anchor chain or hawse hemp rope would pass down the gun deck along both sides of the galley, then through the anchor chain pots and down to the bitter end iron purchase on the keelson near the mainmast keel step. As the deck planks were not in place on the model to support these chains, I thought the chains hanging down between each successive gun deck beam would seem to clutter the deck and not be attractive for the viewer's eye. I therefore shortened their course. The metal ring attachment of the anchor was made from a piece of 3/8-in. brass mast ring. The mast ring was initially cut with a jeweler's saw and the cut ends were then "freshened" with a small flat file to make them smooth. After the oak stock was placed on the shank, this ring was inserted into the hole in the anchor shank and attached to the anchor chain. The ring was then soldered. To stabilize the anchor on its pad, the large tackle from the cathead was secured to this ring via a guide tackle from the timberheads. This guide tackle could also be used to activate the anchor releasing device as in Fig. 71(B). On the

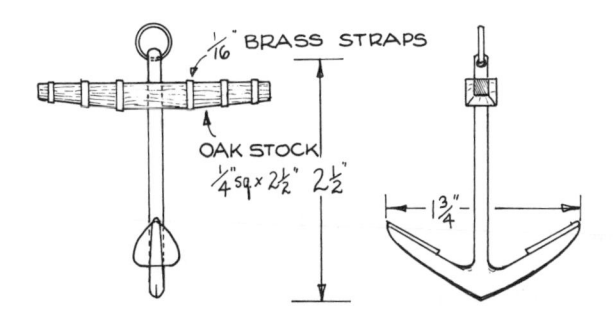

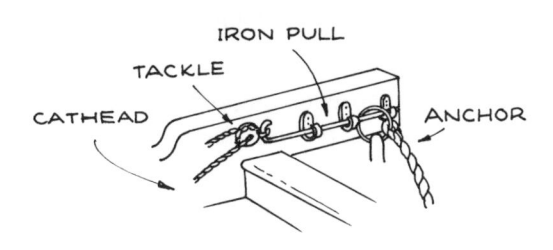

Fig. 71. Anchor, (A), and anchor releasing device, (B)

Constellation, this device was made from three small eyebolts. As noted, all engaged with a small brass (iron) bolt—when this bolt was pulled back the engaged anchor chain was released subsequently dropping the anchor. These guide tackles were also utilized to facilitate controlling the anchor as it was pulled from the water by the capstan.

The plank-sheer for the remainder of the vessel was constructed from 1/16-in. cherry stock cut to fit the curvature of each successive bulwark: forward, aft, spar deck, gangway bulwark, and curved stern pieces. The curved shape was easily obtained by holding the wood to be cut over the top wale of the ship and marking or scoring its underside with a pencil. These pieces were then cut to size, the edges gently rounded, and then scarfed together. As the plank-sheer is obviously large, approximately six pieces were needed to complete the plank-sheer to the midline of the stern. These were straight scarfs, unmorticed, and the edges were epoxied together. They were given a finishing coat of shellac and clear spar varnish prior to gluing in place. The "end plank" was made in a similar fashion from 1/16-in. cherry as shown in Fig. 72. On the *Constellation* there are presently no end plank pieces at the ends of the fore and aft spardeck bulwarks. It was the custom, as far as I have been able to determine, to prevent exposing the bulwark and grain oak planking to the vargaries of the sea and weather by overclosing the butt end of each bulwark with a wooden cover. I do not frankly know if these wooden pieces plan to be added to the *Constellation* in Baltimore's Inner Harbor as they are in place on the *Constitution* in Boston Harbor. (The *Constitution* end planks additionally have inlay carved surfaces which I felt compelled to add to my model; they quickly added an attractive appearance to the staggered segmental plank-sheer.)

Spar Deck Fittings

We are now to the point of considering construction of some of the final spar deck fittings before looking forward to the "grand finale" of construction—the mast, spars, and rigging of the model in the next chapters.

Skylights. There are three skylights in the aft spar deck, two aft of the mizzenmast over the captain's quarters and one aft of the captain's anteroom. These provided some light to the obviously dreary below deck area, especially the captain's quarters. These skylights were constructed of 1/8-in.-by-1/16-in. walnut stock as note in Fig. 73. The

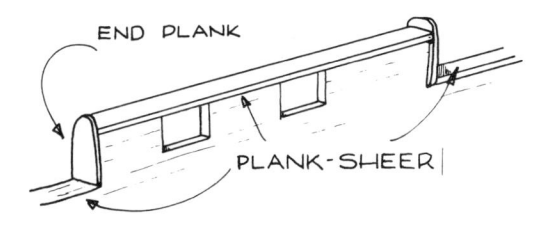

Fig. 72. Plank-sheer and end plank

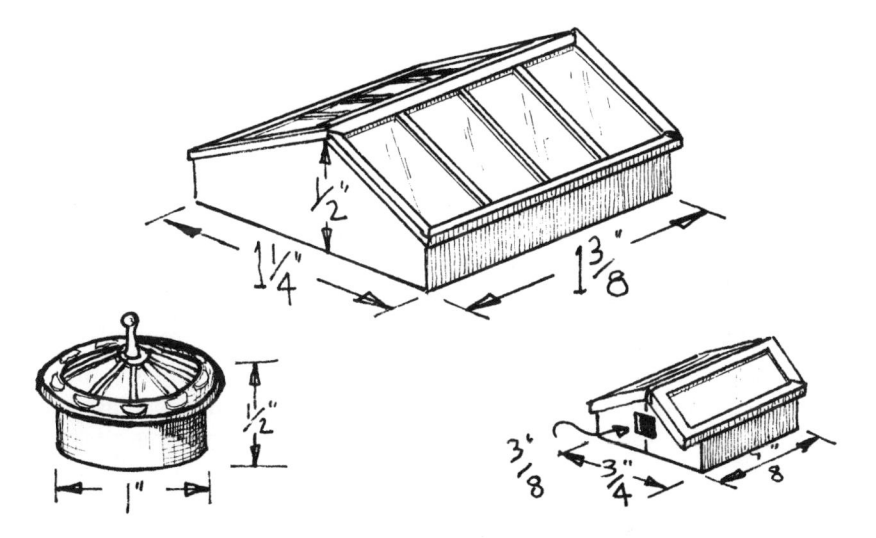

Fig. 73. Skylights

windows were made from a 3/32-in. thickness of Celluloid or Plexiglas film. These were easily constructed and glued in place with dimensions as noted (Fig. 73).

Binnacle. The binnacle was made from 1/4-in.-by-1/8-in. cherry stock. The top was a solid Plexiglas piece fashioned in the shape of the compass cover with a gold scored circle painted on the bottom of the Plexiglas to simulate the compass (Fig. 74), and was stationed immediately aft of the steering wheel. There appears to be some question as to where the binnacle was situated on the *Constellation*. On the vessel in Baltimore, it has been situated forward of the mizzenmast which may be a temporary placement. Functionally, under reasonable weather conditions the compass could be seen by the helmsman. In heavy weather, several helmsman would be required to hold the wheel—at which time an additional helmsman or a midshipman would watch the lighted compass. It is obviously easier to see the binnacle if it is situated next to the steering wheel. On many sailing vessels of this vintage, the binnacle was situated immediately forward of the steering wheel to obviously facilitate the helmsmen's direct vision of the compass.

Belfry. The belfry was placed immediately forward of the fore deck athwartships rail and, on the model, was constructed of wild cherry stock. Its shape is interesting architecturally as it adds a nice baroque appearance and is very pleasing to the eye. It seems interesting that the belfry continued to be somewhat ornate whereas the gingerbread or ornate carvings of large sailing ships began to atrophy approximately one hundred years earlier. The elaborate and extravagant baroque, or neo-baroque, carvings on French, Dutch, and English vessels had been shed at the expense of beauty but at the behest of decreasing the high cost of shipbuilding. In addition to pragmatic economic factors, the loss of ornate carvings reflected the decrease in the need for ostentatious, vain-glorious attempts by kings and rulers to impress one another. Another fact which must be taken into account is the change in cultural taste; as baroque embellishments decreased in

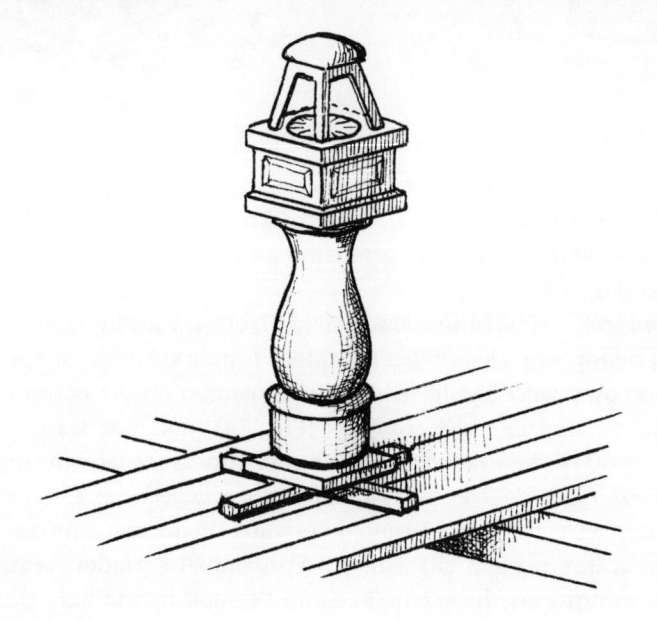

Fig. 74. Binnacle

churches, palaces, and public buildings they also decreased in use on royal vessels of war. At any rate, some of the beauty of the analogue of a church bell enclosure persisted in the construction of the belfry. The bell support was constructed of 1/8-in. cherry stock, and the brass bell was turned from 1/4-in. brass rod and connected to the bell support with a small piece of 1/32-in. wide shim brass wrapping and eyebolt. The cherry wood was finished natural with shellac undercoat and spar varnish exterior. Dimensions are as given in Fig. 75.

Carronades. The carronades for the *Constellation* were 24-pound cannon designed to fire grapeshot or bags of metal cuttings at short ranges to wreak havoc with the sails and humans alike of the opposing vessel. The two-piece wooden base was constructed from 1/8-in. cherry with multiple eyebolts to serve as purchases for the train tackles. The forepart of the carronade carriage was fixed to the lower port sill of its gunport with a small brass rod. Below the lower carriage of the aft portion of the carronade, two wheels or rollers were mounted which enabled the carriage to be rolled from side to side and brought quickly to bear on appropriate targets. The various views of the carriage and carronade are viewed in Figs. 76 and 77. There was a training or sighting screw mounted to the upper baseboard of the carriage which passed through the pommel iron of the carronade. There was also an oblong threaded handle on this vertical screw which enabled one to train the barrel of the carronade up and down to adjust its depth of fire or height of trajectory as needed. I employed a 1/16-in. brass threaded bolt for this purpose and added a small, winglike threaded handle to fit

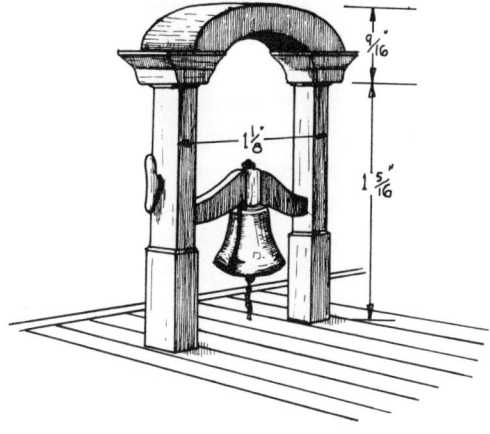

Fig. 75. Belfry

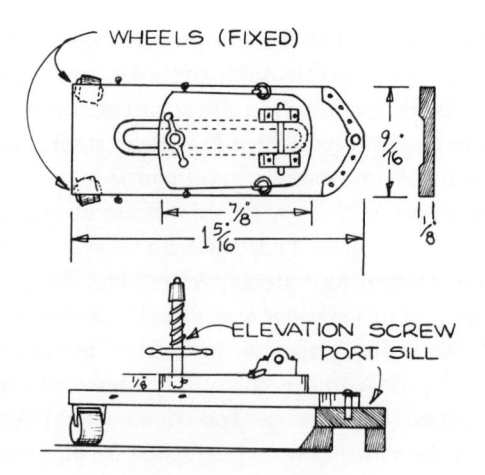

Fig. 76. Twenty-four-pound carronade carriage

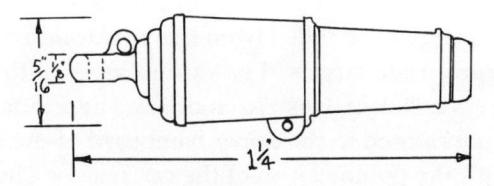

Fig. 77. Twenty-four-pound carronade

this bolt underneath the pommel iron of the carronade (Fig. 77). As there were only six barrels needed, they were all turned brass in contrast to the rubbermold cast method employed with the 18-pound cannons. Two of the carronades were stationed on the fore spar deck and four on the aft spar deck. Only two port and two starboard gunports were utilized on the aft spar deck. This was done for several reasons: (1) not to completely obscure the detail work on the below deck of the captain's quarters and (2) not to "clutter up" the entire aft portion of the open spar deck with gun tackles.

Two training tackles were employed on each side of the carronade cannon and secured to the eyebolts on either side of their respective gunports. These training tackles were similar to those constructed for the 18-pound cannon utilizing a double block purchased to the side of the gunport and a single block secured to the carriage. The carronade did not rest on the carriage with a trunnion in the usual sense in that there was a small piece of iron stock mounted on the bottom of the cannon which was then hinged on the top part of the wooden carriage with an iron pin. There was also a large breech tackle through the iron loop medial to the pommel iron and secured to the bulwark near the gunport with ring eyebolts. The carriage was finished natural with shellac and varnish. The back carriage wheels were constructed of 1/16-in. thick pieces cut from brass rod which was in 3/32 in. in diameter with a brass cover wheel which was in turn mounted to the bottom of the carriage as noted in Fig. 78. The forepart of each carriage was then attached to the lower gunport sill with a brass nail.

Steering Wheel. The last fitting to add to the upper spar deck was the steering wheel. This is the one fitting which cannot be made out of any old wood because it will be subject to continued splitting unless you use hard or tight-grained wood. I, therefore, recommend boxwood if available and, if not, lime, pear, or apple wood that has been adequately dried and selected without checks or splits. As I did not have a large enough piece of boxwood, I used a small piece of well dried apple wood from a nearby orchard to make one of the two rims required for the double steering wheel as noted in Fig. 79. These two woods, when shellacked and varnished, were not identical in color but the slight difference was not enough to detract from the general appearance of the steering wheel.

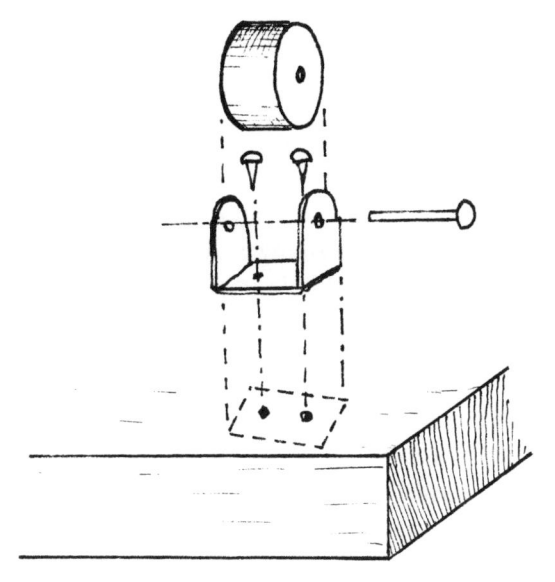

Fig. 78. Wheel mount for twenty-four-pound carronade

Fig. 79. Steering wheel

The rim was initially lathe turned with the outside diameter of the wheel 5/8 in., the width, 1/8 in., and the thickness 3/32 in. A small, 1/32-in. groove was made on the lateral surface of the wheel but obviously it was not possible to complete the groove on both sides while the wood was in the drill-chuck of the lathe. Therefore, after the rim was removed from the lathe, the groove on the back surface of the wheel was hand cut utilizing a small carving knife. A second identical steering wheel was then constructed from apple wood to duplicate the first wheel. The spokes for the wheels were made from orange sticks. As a Naval surgeon during the Vietnam conflict, I was stationed with the Marines at Camp Pendleton, California. The standard fingernail cleaning implements for operating room scrubs were orange sticks which were 1/8 in. to 3/16 in. diameter, always present near the prep or surgical scrub areas. I discovered that these discarded orange sticks were very useful in making ship model fittings and so I used them while working on several plank-on-frame models during my sojourn in the military service, especially for the spokes on the wheel. The diameter was slightly less than 1/16 in. and, although it may be possible to turn these down with a small commercial lathe (for example, a Unimat). I have not found a suitable method to do this with a large lathe utilizing a drill chuck as it is not quite stable enough to prevent vibration with such small diameter wood fittings. In fact, the stanchions or spokes may be cut down to the right outside diameter and then having marked the dimensions with pencil, the spokes may be roll cut and readily carved, obtaining a finished product close to that which may be achieved on the lathe. The wheel was appropriately drilled to accept the spokes and glued to the center drum section of the steering wheel which had been fashioned out of a small piece of oak stock, 3/16 in. in diameter, grooved at each end to accept the spokes. The wheel supports on each side of the wheel were made out of thin Plexiglas as noted in Fig. 79. I attempted to fashion these out of 1/16-in. oak stock which I eventually abandoned as it just did not work well. These were then painted beige color in an attempt to mimic the appearance of varnished oak. Two small brass pins were placed through these frames and inserted into the wheel drums to support the steering wheel. These frames were subsequently glued to the spar deck planking. The drum of the steering wheel was then wrapped with tea-stained linen thread to simulate the hemp rope, reeved through two single blocks which were attached to the spar deck planking and subsequently reeved through a series of two single blocks purchased to the bulwark, one at the level of the underside spar deck and secured one at the level of the underside of the gun deck and then subsequently seized to the eyebolts on each side of the tiller, thus completing the steering wheel attachment to the tiller and allowing one to gently turn the rudder by rotation of the steering wheel.

PART III
PARS AND RIGGING

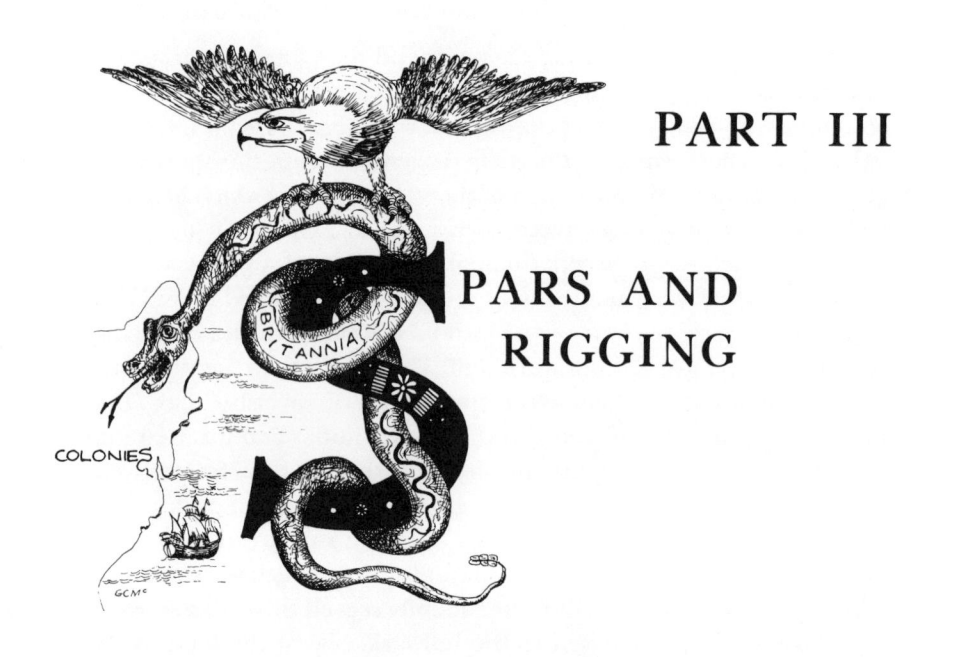

CHAPTER IV
Masts and Spars

Before constructing and stepping the masts of the *Constellation,* I would like to remind the modeller that the three mast steps were fashioned and placed on the keelson prior to the assembly of the frames of each deck and also the orlop, berth, gun and spar decks had mast placement or position marked on the midline planking (Chapter II.). After assembling of the mast, the appropriate holes were fashioned at each deck level, and the tapered or angled mast coats constructed.

Pin Racks and Mast Channels

The pin racks or rails were all the same size in width and thickness, and the number of belaying pins and placement of the pins per rail is as noted in the main plans of the spar deck (Plate III). The pin racks were made of 1/4-in.-by-1/8-in. cherry, tapered and slightly rounded on the inboard side and attached to the bulwark or inner wales with 3/8-in.

MASTS AND SPARS

stainless steel nails after previously drilling through the pin racks and into the bulwarks as noted in Fig. 80.

After completion of the pin racks, the mast channels were constructed of 1/8-in.-by-1/2-in. cherry stock, tapered slightly to the outboard segment, measured, and drilled to accept the deadeye strops. The small holes to accept the attachments from the deadeyes were drilled with a 1/32-in. drill and then squared with a small square file to accept the squared shape of the deadeye strop as noted in Fig. 81. The deadeyes, chains, and chain plates had to be located in such a fashion so that they would not get in the way of the gunport openings as noted in Fig. 82. The channels were tapered slightly inboard so that the channel in abeam or athwartships direction was parallel with the water surface and also to compensate for the angle of the "tumblehome" or inward inclination of the sides of the hull. They were then lightly shellacked, varnished, and attached to the sides of the hull with counterset 1/2-in. small brads, the holes having been previously drilled through the channels and into the bulwarks before nailing home the brads. Obviously, the drilling was to decrease the chance of splitting, against which cherry wood is usually fairly resistant, however. Since as previously noted the planks have already been painted flat black before mounting the channels, we must make sure that all the channels have the holes for the deadeye strops in place prior to insertion of the channel, or gluing the channel onto the hull. The specific length and location of the attachment of the channel to the hull is as noted on the spar deck plans (Plate III). The deadeyes were made from oak and cherry stock. For the models I had made prior to this one, including several of plank-on-frame construction, I had always used commercially available deadeyes, thinking that they would be difficult to make. In fact, the exact opposite is true if one has hardwood available. Boxwood is ideal but

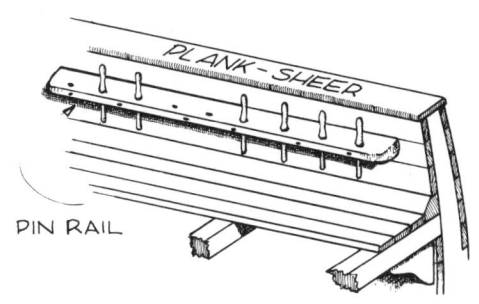

Fig. 80. Belaying pin rack

Fig. 81. Channel construction

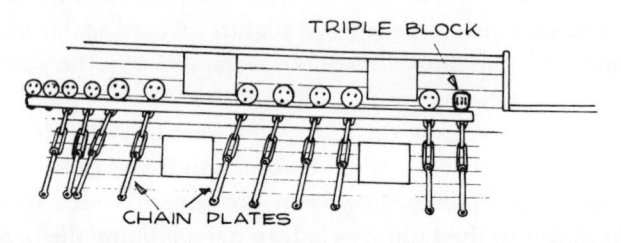

Fig. 82. Chain and chain plates

any hardwood will do. The method is as follows: I carved or spun down a small piece of stock to the desired outside diameter dimension, then drilled three holes 1/32 in. or less in diameter through the end of the dowel which I had fashioned. Then I cut off each segment, and gently rounded the sides in preparation for application of the strop. A small groove can be filed in the circumference of the deadeye with a small needle round file. The strops were made from small cutoff pieces of brass tubing which is usually available at most hobby shops, filed to the desired dimension, and then clenched with pliers as noted in Fig. 83. The dimension of the deadeyes is rather simple: 1/8-in. diameter for the mizzenmast, 5/16-in. diameter for the foremast, 3/8-in. diameter for the mainmast, and the strop material was cut from thin brass tubing of 5/8 in., 1/2 in., and 3/8 in. diameter respectively.

Chain and Chain Plate

Once all of the channels and deadeyes for the main shrouds were in place, the first link of the deadeye chain was inserted through each deadeye strop underneath the channel to keep the deadeyes from literally falling out. I should mention that only the first and second

MASTS AND SPARS 89

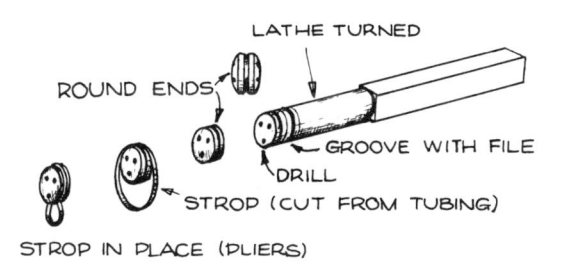

Fig. 83. Deadeyes and strops

deadeyes (one a triple block) with the least fore and aft angle with the mast were chain plated in position before the shroud rigging was in place at the masthead. This was to insure that the angle of the chain plate coincided and was coincident with the angle of the shroud and the mast above the channel. The other chain plates were to be placed and nailed in position after the masts were constructed and glued in place—making the chain plate angle with the channel, plank, and masthead more readily determined. So essentially only the first two chains were attached to their respective chain plates and nailed home in order to secure the channel in place and enable the other shrouds to be attached. After the masts were in place and each successive shroud had been attached, the second chain and the chain plate were stationed on the hull in the same angle as the shroud with the masthead, holes were then drilled in the planking beneath each chain plate, and small brass nails were inserted. This tended to keep the chain plate, chains, and shrouds in a uniform position with obviously the greatest angularity toward the back or aft section of the channel. The chain plates I used in the model were purchased, 7/8 in. by 3/64 in. by 1/16 in. in dimensions although they could be readily made of 1/16-in. brass stock if so desired. I had a chance to visit James Bliss, marine suppliers, while in Boston at a meeting and couldn't resist purchasing the finely finished and polished brass chain plates, making it necessary for me to say that everything on the model was not made from scratch. At any rate, the chains themselves were constructed in a similar way to which the eyebolts of the gun carriages were made: .031 brass wire was wrapped about a piece of oak which was 3/8 in.-by-1/8 in. in size with the edges slightly rounded. [The edge of this wrapped wire was then cut with a small metal saw so that each chain was flat on its cut surface and easily inserted through the strop of each deadeye. The second chain loop could also be easily inserted about the nail of the upper portion of the chain plate.] Additionally, the top part of the chain plate had to be bent with pliers to approximately a 1/32-in. angle in order to accommodate the second chain loop. The chain and chain plate construction are illustrated in Figs. 84 and 85. Each chain piece could have been made by cutting the loop with pliers except the ends of the chain would be tapered with the pliers and not fit well whereas when they are cut with a saw, the segments may be pushed together obtaining a flush joint. The remainder of the chain plates were nailed in place after the shrouds had been fitted to the complete masts.

Mainmast Construction

The masts for the *Constellation* were made from choice logs of white pine and held together with iron bands. On the model, oak may be used, but maple or birch dowel will also do perfectly well. If maple dowel is used, diameters are: 5/8 in. for the foremast, 3/4 in. for the

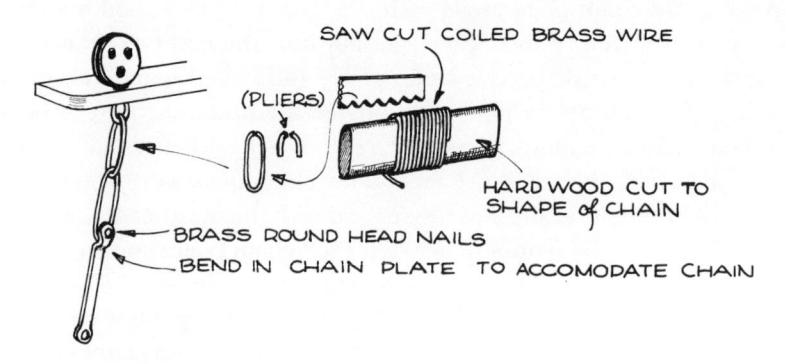

Fig. 84. Method of chain construction

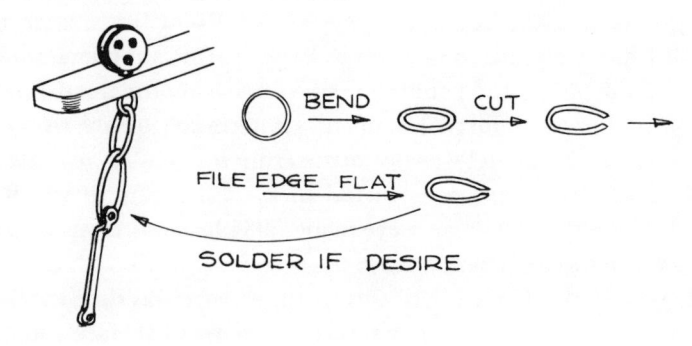

Fig. 85. Alternative method of chain construction

MASTS AND SPARS

mainmast, and 1/2 in. for the mizzenmast. These standard sizes are close to real scale once they have been cut and tapered to the proper dimensions. The method of construction for each mast is similar so that the detailed description of the mainmast will readily suffice for all three masts. It should be mentioned that each entire mast should be constructed, including the mast tops and caps prior to incorporation into the model. The dimensions of the masts, mast tops, crosstrees, bowsprit, and spars are listed in the series of Tables I through V.

The full-size dimensions of the mainmast are as noted in Fig. 86. All of the mast bands were made from overlapped 3/32-in. wide brass, painted black, and positioned after the mast had been painted white and before the rubbing paunch was in place. During the discussion of the construction of the masts and spars, occasionally the full-size foot dimensions may be given, however, obviously it is easy to convert 1 ft to a 1/4-in. scale for model construction as necessary.

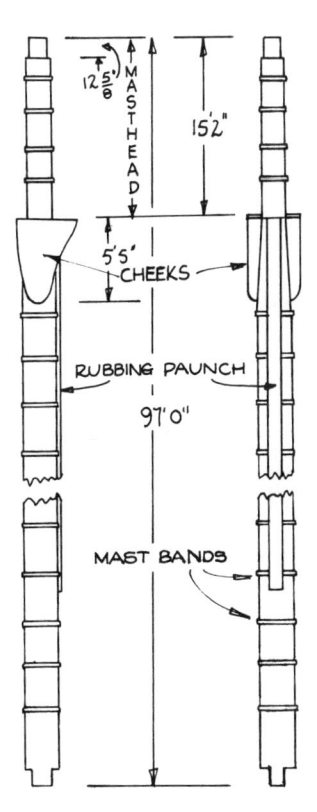

Fig. 86. Mainmast

When I made a plank-on-frame model of the HMS *Victory*, I was able to pick up a copy of C. Nepean Longridge's book, *The Anatomy of Nelson's Ships* in which I found reference to Steel's classic work, *The Elements of Mast Making, Sail Making and Rigging* (see Bibliography). I was able to purchase an old copy of Steel and recommend it for anyone who intends to spend any time at all on model ship building. From my reading I learned that the common source for all spar sizes is the size of the mainmast which may be obtained from a very simple equation. Specifically, the length of the mainmast equals the extreme beam plus the gun deck length divided by two:

$$\text{Length mainmast} = \frac{\text{extreme beam} + \text{gun deck length}}{2}$$

From the length of this mainmast, the following spar length dimensions may be obtained:

Foremast, 8/9 length of the mainmast
Mizzenmast, 6/7 length of mainmast
Main topmast, 3/5 length of mainmast
Fore topmast, 8/9 length of main topmast
Mizzen topmast, 3/4 length of main topmast
Topgallant mast, 1/2 length of corresponding topmast
Bowsprit, 7/11 length of mainmast

And the length of yards may also be obtained as follows:

Main, 8/9 of mainmast
Fore, 7/8 of main yard
Mizzen, 6/7 of main yard
Main topsail, 5/7 of main yard
Fore-topsail, 7/8 of main topsail yard
Mizzen topsail, 2/3 of main topsail yard
Crossjack, same as fore-topsail yard
Top gallant, 2/3 of its topsail yard
Spritsail, same as fore-topsail yard

Prior to explaining the particulars of spar construction, I have a "carpentry" hint or two. There are several ways to cut the mast to size—one can turn it on a lathe and therefore readily taper it accordingly to the proper dimensions, or one can round carve it from a square or round piece of stock. The easier method is to obtain a properly dimensioned hardwood dowel, oak, lance, maple, or birch and then carve it to the appropriate tapered size. With square stock, one may start by cutting off the corners so to speak, changing the 4 sides to 8, then to 16, and then subsequently to round. The especially helpful maneuver which I learned in my youth by accident while attempting to reproduce a Ute Indian arrow which I had seen in a museum in the basement of the capital building in Salt Lake City, Utah, is a specific technique which has obviously been around for centuries. It is to scrape down the wood by holding a sharp knife at a 90° angle to the wood in a similar fashion to scraping the skin off carrots. The easiest blade to use is an X-acto blade or sharpened pocket knife. Commercial scalpel blades are too thin and break too readily for repeated use.

Cheeks, Bibs, and Mast Tops. After the masthead had been carved square, the cheeks, bibs, and mast tops were constructed. The mast cheeks were cut from 1/8-in. oak, and the superior border angled according to the rake of the mast given previously. It is important to maintain this slope carefully so that when completed and the mast is in place, the mast top is parallel to the water's surface. The rakes of the mast are again noted here for convenience: mainmast, 3/4 in. to 1 ft; foremast, 9/16 in. to 1 ft; and mizzenmast, 1-1/8 in. to 1 ft.

Once the cheeks were in place, the trestletrees were made from 5/16-in.-by-3/16-in. oak, cut to size, notched to accommodate the crosstrees, and glued and nailed in place. Once again, it is important that the trestletrees be correctly lined up, not only to fit the crosstrees but in the same plane so that when the mast top is fitted over the finished cross and trestletree system, it is level or parallel to the water. Birch wood, 1/4-in. rounded, was used to form a bolster, and placed on the trestletrees in the midline. The bolsters were utilized to decrease chafe of the shrouds. The mast tops were constructed of 1/8-in.-by-1/16-in. oak or basswood planking. This size planking served both for the planking and the rib supports. Fig. 87 is a top view of the mast top. Fig. 88 demonstrates side and front or end views of the mast top.

The various dimensions of the mast tops or, so-called, "fighting tops," of each mast are keyed from the drawings shown in Figs. 87, 88, and 89 alphabetically and correspond to the dimensions given in Table II. The rim of the mast top was constructed out of 1/16-in. thick basswood, and the tapered ribs were glued and butted on this rim. A small square hole was cut out in front of the lubber's hole as noted on the plans through which would pass the yard slings. A small, 1/16-in.-

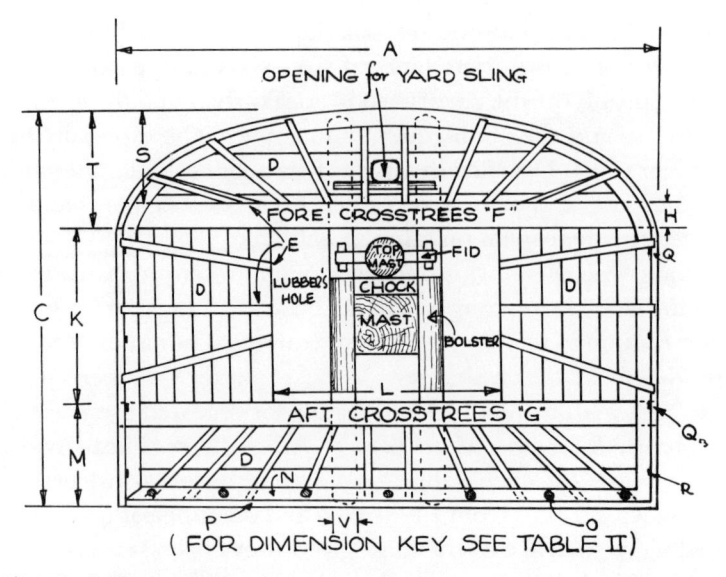

Fig. 87. Typical mast top

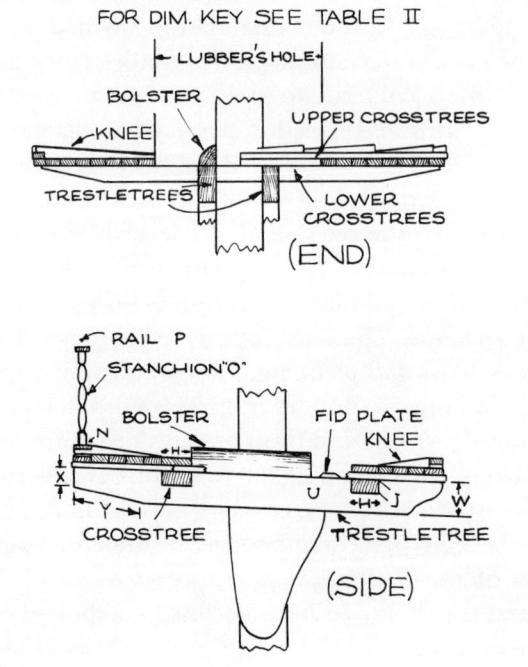

Fig. 88. Mast top

MASTS AND SPARS

BLACK
WHITE
(DIMENSIONS in TEXT)

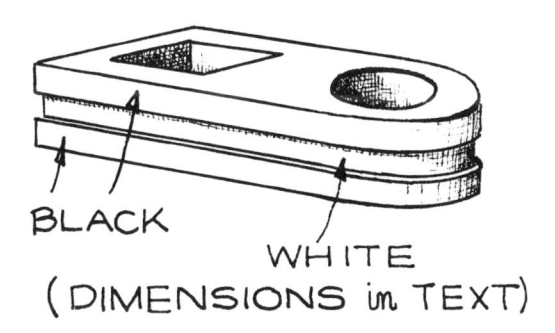

Fig. 89. Mast cap

by-1/2-in. bolster, with one rounded edge, was glued on the aft border of this aperture to functionally decrease chafe on the yard sling ropes. Appropriately position holes were drilled and squared with a file for the top mast deadeye strops near the lateral aspects of port and starboard mast top rim.

Rail Stanchions and Mast Caps. The rail stanchions were carved from 1/8-in. orange stick and the rail top of 1/8-in.-by-1/16-in. oak strip glued in place. Chock pieces, 1/8-in. thick, were placed forward of the masthead, between the trestletrees, to serve as a bumper between the mainmast and the topmast sections. Small, 1/32-in. thick, smooth brass plates were cut, 3/32-in.-by-1/4-in. in size, painted black, and glued in place on the trestletrees forward of the bolsters to serve as fid plates for the cross timbers through the bottom of the topmast and to serve as firm supports to hold or "take the weight" of the topmast on the trestletrees. The mast cap was constructed of oak although it may be more readily constructed of Plexiglas or plastic which oviates the problem of splitting the small oak pieces which have to be drilled and filed during construction. The general shape of the mast caps are as noted in Fig. 89. The dimensions of the mast caps are: fore, 1-1/4 in. by 11/16 in. by 1/4 in.; main, 1-3/8 in. by 3/4 in. by 1/4 in.; mizzen, 1 in. by 1/2 in. by 3/16 in. The square hole aft and the round hole forward in the cap should be angled to keep the mast cap parallel to the mast top. The square hole aft should fit snugly on the masthead for good support. The forward hole of the cap should allow the varnished topmast to pass through its aperture without difficulty. Once again, with the exception of the wooden mast platform or mast top, all spars and caps, trestletrees, and crosstrees should be painted before each mast segment is glued together. The mast cap should be painted with the upper and lower borders flat black and the recessed central portion flat white. The multiple mast bands were made as noted in Fig. 90 from 3/32-in. cut shim brass, painted black, and nailed in position after the mast had been painted. The easiest way to cut and fit the mast bands is to hold them temporarily in place, drill a hole through both band ends as noted in Fig. 90, paint the bands black, and then insert a nail into the previously drilled holes, drive it home and finally give a touch-up with black paint to the tops of the nail heads. This insures a good, clear, well-demarcated junction of the black band with the white mast. After completion of the mainmast platform, the topmast and topgallant mast were constructed (Fig. 91), including the crosstrees and trestletrees.

Crosstrees

The crosstrees in this particular instance were made of wild cherry as there is less splitting. The dimensions of the topmast crosstrees for each individual mast, given in Table III, are letter keyed to coincide with Fig. 92(A) and (B). Bolsters of 1/8 in. were also used similar to the mainmast and a 3/32-in. chock inserted between the topmast and the topgallant mast to maintain positional separation. The topmast was varnished, the crosstrees and trestletrees were painted white, and the varnished topgallant mast was attached and epoxied in place after its flat black mast cap had been made out of 3/16-in. angle-drilled Plexiglas. The last parts of each mast to be completed were the rubbing paunches which were attached to the fore section of each lower mast, the mainmast being 3/32-in.-by-1/4-in. basswood; the foremast, 1/4 in.

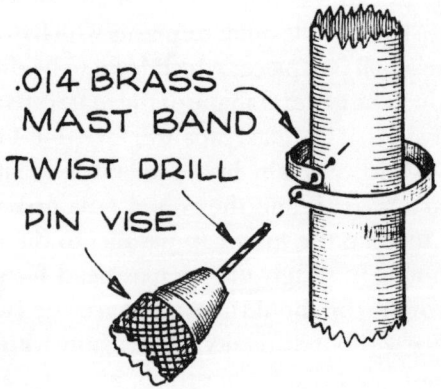

Fig. 90. Mast band

MASTS AND SPARS

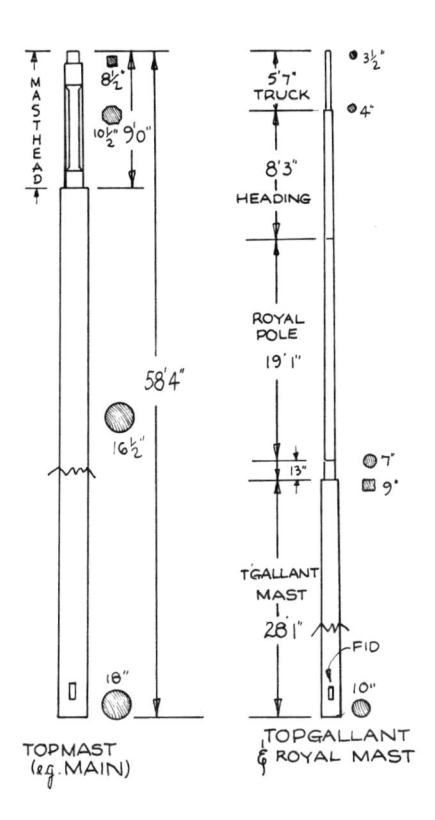

Fig. 91. Typical topmast or mainmast, topgallant, and royal mast

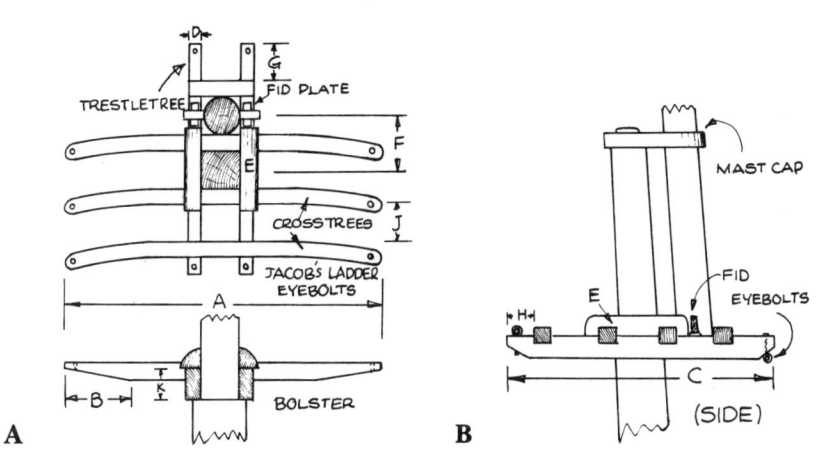

Fig. 92. Topmast crosstrees, typical arrangement, (A), and side view, (B)

by 1/16 in.; and the mizzenmast, 1/8 in. by 1/16 in. These paunches were notched for each mast band already in place and then painted white, glued, and nailed in place with the nail heads being subsequently touched up with white paint.

Mast Coats

Once the fore, main, and mizzenmast were constructed, they were fitted to their respective mast steps with appropriate drilling and shaping of each successive deck to insure proper fit. The circular mast coats, as noted in Fig. 93, were constructed out of Plexiglas for each mast at each deck level and file tapered to accommodate the different rakes. I would encourage the modeller to use Plexiglas, or plastic, as small oak or basswood pieces split very readily when attempting to make tapered mast coats and do not allow reasonable construction. There is another method which I learned while making Fisher body model cars, and subsequently employed on ship models which is to place beeswax or crayon coating over the wood which, in this case would be the mast, and then cover the area with a rim of plastic wood, inclined slightly to coincide with the rake of each individual mast. After this plastic wood dries, it can be easily slipped off the round mast and carved to the desired shape, touching up any inner angulation necessary with files. This method is somewhat cumbersome in view of the large sizes of the masts of this model, however, it is a good thing to remember when making smaller fittings out of plastic wood.

Once all the mast coats were constructed and painted black, all three masts were set up in their mast steps with each deck's mast coats in place, making sure that each mast lined up properly with its mate fore and aft and appropriately raked. A convenient method of gluing each mast with multiple coats to contend with is to initially only glue the mast base in place in its keelson step. After the mast has been stepped and firmly glued onto the keelson, the mast coats then may be progressively slid and lodged into position between each deck and glued in their respective positions.

Bowsprit

After completing the mast, I constructed the bowsprit to correspond with the given dimensions in Table IV. Once again, the bowsprit including jibboom and flying jibboom were finished, painted, and varnished before being permanently positioned in the model.

MASTS AND SPARS 99

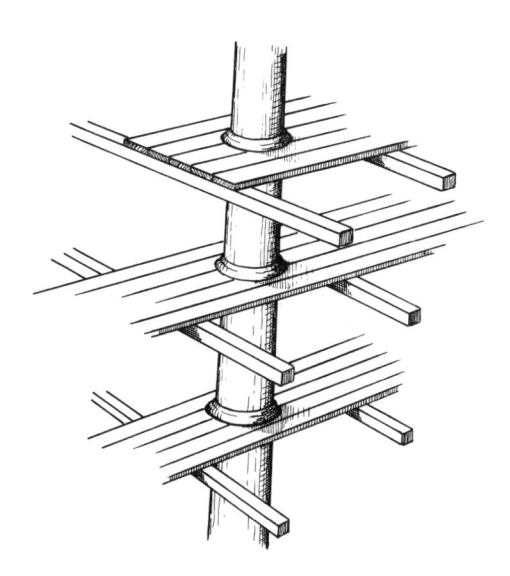

Fig. 93. Mast coats

The main bowsprit was constructed of a piece of 5/8-in. birch dowel, the inboard section of which was planed or carved to the octagon shape as noted in Fig. 59. The bowsprit cap, which attached the jibboom to the bowsprit, was made of 1/4-in. Plexiglas, its attachment noted in Fig. 94. The right side of the bowsprit cap was notched to accept the base of the flying jibboom. The flying jibboom was held in position on the cap with a small piece of shim brass, 3/32 in. wide, which had bolts into the boom and two small bolts simulated by brass nails drilled and inserted into the cap around the base of the boom (Fig. 94). There are two side cheeks on the bowsprit which have been mounted in

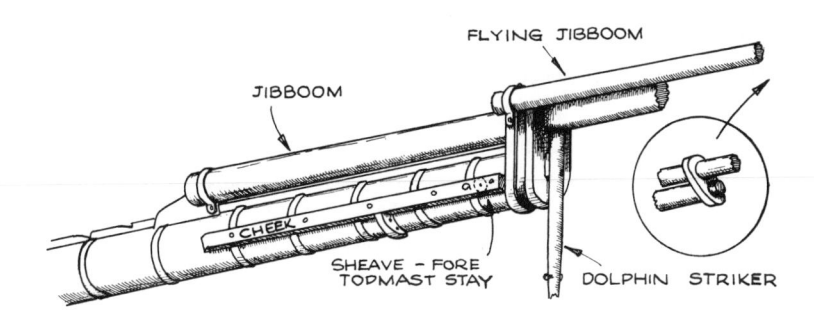

Fig. 94. Bowsprit detail

place and contain several eyebolts for attaching the foremost stays which were constructed of 1/8-in.-by-1/8-in. oak and fitted in place. These cheeks also contain a sheave in their foremost part through which reeves the fore-topmast stay. The jibboom cap which attached the flying jibboom to the jibboom was made of 1/8 in. thick Plexiglas, drilled to fit the distal end of the jibboom and midsection of the flying jibboom. Prior to construction and assembly each piece of bowsprit was painted: the bowsprit flat white, the bands flat black, and the jibboom and flying jibboom natural varnish with shellac undercoat. The bowsprit bands, similar to the mast bands, were made of 3/32-in. shim brass and held in place with small flat head brass nails. This was done before the side cheeks (notched for each band, also) were glued in place. The three or four bands on the octagonal section of the bowsprit may have to be left off in order that the bowsprit may be fitted through the hole in the bulwark and then reattached after the bowsprit has been inserted onto the gun deck. This is obviously dependent on the tightness of the fit of the particular bowsprit with the bowsprit entrance aperture.

A piece of 3/32-in.-by-1/4-in. basswood, slightly notched to fit with the bowsprit bands, and then angle notched on top to simulate steps, was painted flat white and glued in position on the upper surface of the bowsprit from the bowsprit cap to the bow bulwark (Fig. 94).

The dolphin striker was constructed with a piece of 1/4-in. birch dowel, tapered, painted white, and glued into place. There are several small brass fairleads and eyebolts which are attached to this structure and epoxied permanently in place.

Yards

As mentioned previously, representative yards will be discussed and the other yard construction may be readily based on the information from construction of these several yards. The main yard was constructed from 5/8-in. birch dowel. The center octagonal section may be carved for this model although the standard method would be to taper or curve it to its octagonal shape and apply wooden battens which strengthen the center section of the yard. The battens, yard slings, horses, jack stays, and stirrups are all shown in Fig. 95. The lower two yards of each mast were battened with eight small planks, added in octagonal fashion to the midsection of the yard as previously mentioned. On the model, these may be made from 1/16-in., 1/4-in., 3/16-in. basswood as noted (Fig. 95). The square battens, 1 through 4, could be added initially followed by the tapered battens, 4 through 8.

MASTS AND SPARS 101

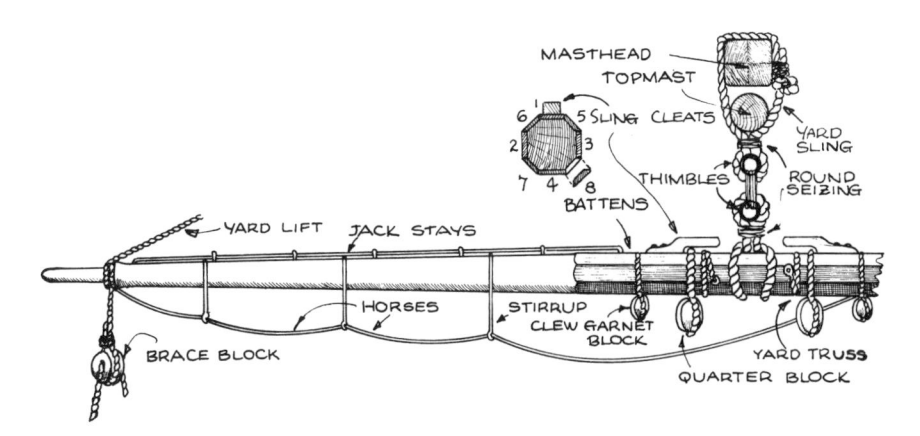

Fig. 95. Main yard

The top sling cleat is also included. As mentioned, these battens are customary on the main and top sail yards of each mast of vessels of this vintage (the lower mizzen yard is also called the crossjack yard). The small sling cleats are visually self-explanatory and were constructed of 1/4-in.-by-1/8-in. oak stock. The yard slings and trusses will be described under rigging (Chapter VI). The jack stays, stirrups, and horses are as noted in Fig. 95. The jack stay rods on top of the yards were made of .012-in. piano wire, mounted at regular intervals with small brass eyebolts with the ends bent at right angles and fixed into the wood of the mast through small drilled holes in the center section and distal portion of each yard. The stirrups were made from brass wire, .012 in. (Fig. 95). The jack stay ropes or horses were made with white linen thread, #40 commercial size. The ropes were stained with tea to obtain the beige or appropriate light tan color. On the vessel these horses were utilized by the crew as footholds and supports while reefing or furling sail. The clew garnet and quarter blocks were placed on the main yards. However, the leech and buntline blocks were not added to the lower yards as sails were not going to be placed in accordance with the custom for full-rigged models of this scale.

A typical upper mast yard, or topgallant, and royal yard are similar to the main yard except that there are no battens on them. The wooden equivalent of the more modern iron trusses which attach the yard to the mast are shown in Fig. 96. The truss connectors (closed cleats) on these yards were made from 3/32-in.-by-1/4-in. oak and were fitted with eyebolts or were drilled with two holes to receive the ropes from the yard parrals which enabled the yards to be moved up and down

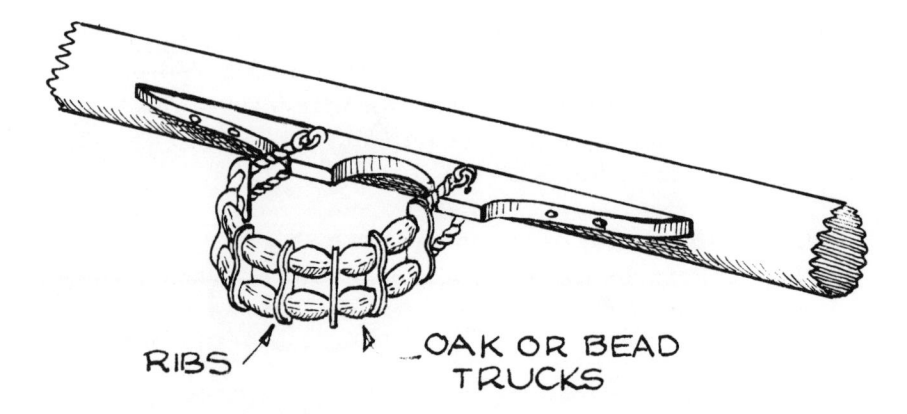

Fig. 96. Yard and parral

(Fig. 96). The parrals were constructed of small black beads or could be constructed of 3/32-in. dowel which was tapered on both ends, cut off in small segments, and drilled centrally with 1/32-in. drill. The parral ribs were made of 1/32-in. oak or Plexiglas. The black beads if used for trucks, should be painted flat black.

Gaff and Spanker Booms

After completion of the yards, I made the gaff and spanker booms of 1/4-in. dowel, tapering the gaff boom with the snow mast as noted in Fig. 97. The snow mast, a small mast, was fitted aft of the mizzenmast and mounted on a chock between aft mizzen trestletrees and the spar deck below near the mizzenmast foot. The boom and gaff were attached to this snow mast with small parrals to move more efficiently

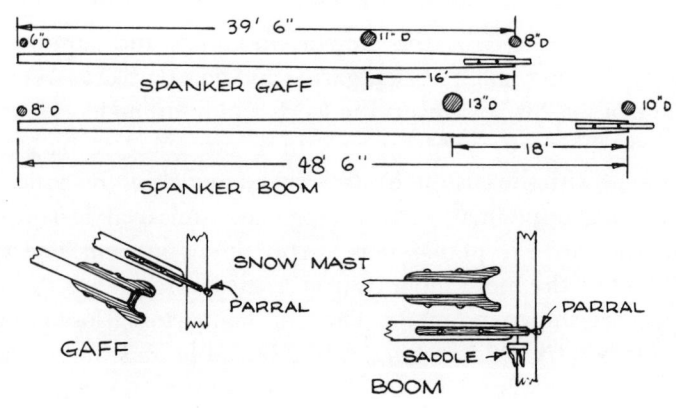

Fig. 97. Spanker gaff and boom

MASTS AND SPARS

with tacking. On the model the snow mast was constructed from 3/16-in. birch dowel. The gaff boom and spanker boom were finished natural with spar varnish. The yards were painted flat black including the spritsail yard and the yardarms were painted flat white prior to attachment to the masts.

Table I. Mast Dimensions

(The dimensions for this and the following tables, Table II-Table V, are given in feet but can be readily converted to model scale of 1/4 in. to 1 foot.)

Key	Fore Length Ft. In.	Fore Dia. In.	Main Length Ft. In.	Main Dia. In.	Mizzen Length Ft. In.	Mizzen Dia. In.
Lower Mast (Full Length)	89 4	29½	97 0	32	83 4	23
Lower Masthead	13 11	20	15 2	22	10 2	17
Topmast (overall)	53 6	18	58 4	18	42 6	13
Topmast Masthead	8 4	10¼	9 0	10½	6 9	7½
Topgallant Mast	25 8	9	28 1	10	20 6	8
Royal Mast (pole)	18 1	6	19 1	7	14 2	5
Heading	8 0	5	8 3	6	6 4	4
Truck	5 7	3	5 7	3½	3 10	2½

Table II. Mast Top Dimensions

(Calculated from Topmast Length—After Polland)

Key		Fore	Main	Mizzen
A	Length of 1/3 topmast	17 ft. 10 in.	19 ft. 6 in.	14 ft. 2 in.
C	Length of 1/4 topmast	13 ft. 4 in.	14 ft. 7 in.	10 ft. 7 in.
D	Boarding (planks)	3 in. × 6 in.	3 in. × 6 in.	3 in. × 6 in.
E	Knees tapered	6 in. × 4 in.	6 in. × 4 in.	6 in. × 4 in.
F	Length forward crosstrees	17 ft. 8 in.	19 ft. 6 in.	14 ft. 2 in.
G	Length aft crosstrees	17 ft. 8 in.	19 ft. 6 in.	14 ft. 2 in.
H	Width crosstrees	9¼ in.	10¼ in.	7½ in.
I	Depth crosstrees	6¼ in.	6⅞ in.	5⅛ in.
K	Center square	6 ft. 7½ in.	7 ft. 3 in.	5 ft. 3 in.
L	Center square (athwart)	7 ft. 1 in.	7 ft. 10 in.	5 ft. 8 in.
M	Aft crosstress	2 ft. 8 in.	2 ft. 11 in.	2 ft. 1 in.

(*Continued*)

Table II. Mast Top Dimensions (*Continued*)

Key		Fore	Main	Mizzen
N	Stanchion board	1¼ in. × 7 in.	1¼ in. × 7 in.	1¼ in. × 7 in.
O	Stanchions	3 in. × 5 in.	3 in. × 5 in.	3 in. × 5 in.
P	Stanchion rail	3 in. × 5 in.	3 in. × 5 in.	3 in. × 5 in.
Q	Foremost futtock hole	aft of topmast		
R	Aftermost futtock hole	6 ft.	6 ft.	6 ft.
S	Forepart of top to crosstree	3 ft. 3 in.	3 ft. 6¼ in.	2 ft. 7½ in.
T	S & H*	4 ft. 0 in.	4 ft. 4½ in.	3 ft. 9½ in.
U	Length of trestletrees	12 ft. 10 in.	14 ft. 1 in.	10 ft. 1 in.
V	Width of trestletrees	9¼ in.	10¼ in.	7½ in.
W	Depth of trestletrees	14 in.	15¼ in.	11 in.
X	Shaft trestletrees	7 in.	7½ in.	5½ in.
Y	Shape total aft trestletrees	20 in.	21¾ in.	15½ in.

* S is forepart of top to crosstree; H is width of crosstrees.

Table III. Topmast Crosstree Dimensions

Key		Fore Ft.	Fore In.	Main Ft.	Main In.	Mizzen Ft.	Mizzen In.
A	Length crosstrees	5	5	6	2	5	2
B	Angle underside crosstrees		17½		20½		16
C	Length trestletrees	4	9	5	1	4	3
D	Thickness trestletrees		4		4		4
E	Bolster		5		5		5
F	Centerline of topmast to topgallant mast		14½		15½		3¼
G	Fore trestletree to chock dimension		4¼		5		3½
H	Aft trestletree		5¾		6		4½
J	Between second and third crosstree		8		9		7
K	Width trestletrees		7		7		6

Table IV. Bowsprit Dimensions

	Length	Diameter
Bowsprit	51 ft. 7⅞ in.	30⅝ in.
Jibboom	49 ft. 8 in.	19 in.
Flying Jibboom	54 ft. 3 in.	9½ in.

Table V. Spar Dimensions

	Fore Length Ft.	Fore Length In.	Fore Dia. In.	Main Length Ft.	Main Length In.	Main Dia. In.	Mizzen Length Ft.	Mizzen Length In.	Mizzen Dia. In.
Lower yard	80	2	18	92	6	21	60	11	16
Topsail yard	60	7	12½	68	10	15	44	11	10
Topgallant yard	37	5	10	37	6	10	27	8	7¾
Royal yard	24	6	6½	27	8	7	18	3	5
Spanker boom							48	6	13
Spanker Gaff							39	6	11
Spritsail yard (bowsprit)	60	3	12						

Table VI. Belaying Pin and Eyebolt Position
(For Numbers: See Plate III)

Belaying Pin	Eyebolt Position	Specific Rigging
	1	Fore topgallant stay (port)
	2	Jibboom martingale stay (port)
	3	Jibboom martingale stay (starboard)
	4	Flying jibboom martingale stay (starboard)
	5	Fore topmast preventer stay (port)
	6	Fore topmast stay (starboard)
	7	Fore topmast preventer stay (port-timberhead)
	8	Fore topmast stay (starboard-timberhead)
9		Flying jibstay (starboard)
10		Fore royal stay (port)

(Continued)

Table VI. Belaying Pin and Eyebolt Position (*Continued*)

Belaying Pin	Eyebolt Position	Specific Rigging
	11	Jibstay
	12 & 13	Spritsail truss (p & s)
14 & 15		Spritsail lifts (p & s)
16 & 17		Spritsail braces (p & s)
	18 to 23	Fore, main, and mizzen "swifters" shrouds; (falls to eyebolts in channel)
24	24 to 30	Bentinck shrouds
	31	Main topmast preventer stay (starboard)
	32	Main topmast stay (port)
	33	Mizzen topgallant stay (eyebolt)
	34	Mizzen royal stay (starboard)
	35	Main topgallant stay (port)
	36	Main royal stay (starboard)
	37	Lower foreyard truss (cleats on foremast bitts)
38 & 39		Lower foreyard lifts (p & s)
40 & 41		Lower foreyard braces (p & s)
42 & 43		Fore topsail yard lifts (p & s)
44 & 45	44 & 45	Fore topsail halyard (p & s channel, deck eyebolt, and pin rack)
46 & 47		Fore topsail braces (p & s)
48 & 49		Fore topgallant yard lift (p & s)
50	50	Fore topgallant halyard (starboard, channel, and pin rack)
51 & 52		For topgallant yard brace (p & s)
53 & 54		Fore royal yard lifts (p & s)
55	55	Fore royal yard halyard (port channel and pin rack)
56 & 57		Fore royal yard brace (p & s)
	58	Main yard truss (cleats on mainmast bitts)
59 & 60		Main yard lifts (p & s)
61 & 62		Main braces (cleats)

Belaying Pin	Eyebolt Position	Specific Rigging
63 & 64		Main topsail yard lifts (p & s)
65 & 66	65 & 66	Main topsail halyard (p & s channel and pin rack)
67 & 68		Main topsail braces (p & s)
69 & 70		Main topgallant yard lifts (p & s)
71	71	Main topgallant yard halyard (starboard channel and pin rack)
72 & 73		Main topgallant braces (p & s)
74 & 75		Main royal yard lifts (p & s)
76	76	Main royal yard halyard (port channel and pin rack)
77 & 78		Main royal yard braces (p & s)
	79	Mizzen lower yard truss (cleats mizzen bitts)
80 & 81		Mizzen lower yard lifts (p & s)
82 & 83		Mizzen lower yard braces (p & s)
84 & 85		Mizzen topsail lifts (p & s)
86	86	Mizzen topsail halyard (starboard channel and pin rack)
87 & 88		Mizzen topsail braces (p & s)
89 & 90		Mizzen topgallant yard lifts (p & s)
91	91	Mizzen topgallant yard halyard (starboard channel and pin rack)
92 & 93		Mizzen topgallant yard braces (p & s)
94 & 95		Mizzen royal yard lifts (p & s)
96	96	Mizzen royal yard halyard (port channel and pin rack)
97 & 98		Mizzen royal yard braces (p & s)
99		Spanker gaff peak halyard (p & s)
100		Spanker gaff throat halyard
101 & 102	101 & 102	Spanker gaff vangs (p & s eyebolt and pin rack)
103 & 104	103 & 104	Spanker boom topping lifts (p & s deck eyebolt and pin rack)
105		Guy pendant (traveller rod p & s bulwark cleats)

CHAPTER V
Standing Rigging

We have now come to that part of ship modelling which represents the awe inspiring appearance of large sailing craft and which also demands ingenuity and precision of model construction. As an amateur sailor, I have never been able to learn enough about rigging and sailing, and with each new book I read I realize how slowly knowledge of sailing proceeds. As with so many of man's endeavors, it must be tempered by firsthand experience.

To begin with, standing rigging refers to the stationary mast and bowsprit supports while running rigging refers to the movable ropes, which are reeved through blocks, and move the yards and booms. Usually the fixed or standing rigging is wrapped and tarred and black in color while the running rigging is natural, weathered beige, or a light tan color.

Rope Types and Sizes

The ropes used in vessels of the *Constellation* era were Manila hemp. Most modelists use standard cotton or linen thread undyed or dyed to meet whatever necessity demands. Linen is far superior to cotton as it has much greater longevity and does not stretch and fray as does cotton. Untreated silk is sometimes heat labile and also stretches. On this model, unlike most modellers, I used a fair amount of silk because as a surgeon I had ready access to discarded surgical silk suture material. Therefore, I used surgical numbers when referring to rope size while the commercial equivalent was given as necessary. For example, a #3-0 silk suture is equivalent to #50 thread, either spun or braided, in the textile industry. Also, most surgical silk is manufactured black, hence automatically ideal for standing rigging. Most of the running

STANDING RIGGING

rigging was linen including the jack stay horses, but some cotton rigging was also utilized.

Rope sizes on major rigged vessels were given in circumference rather than diameter which may serve as a source of confusion when you first review full-sized rigged vessel plans and in our discussion of rigging each rope's *actual* circumference will be used. Most ropes were made from vegetable fibers,—hemp, cotton, flax, etc.—and usually made up of three strands. Hawser laid rope is three left-twisted strands and cable or cable-laid rope is usually three right-twisted ropes. Shrouds are usually four strands laid about a central core. Some of the common ways a rope is purchased to blocks, eyebolts, or deadeyes is demonstrated in Fig. 98.

Rope Work Terms. *Seizing* is connecting two ropes together by wrapping them with a smaller piece of rope.

Round seizing is wrapping with a smaller piece of rope around the rope.

Eye seizing is wrapping with a smaller piece of rope around the rope with two cross turns.

Throat seizing has riding turns but no cross turns.

A *becket* is formed when the rope is looped at the end of an eye seizing, usually at the end of a block.

Lashing is serving rope or a cleat, etc., to the rope.

A *strop* is a rope or strap to hold a block in place and enable it to be attached to an eyebolt or another rope.

Worming is laying small rope in the pulleys or valleys between the strands (contlines).

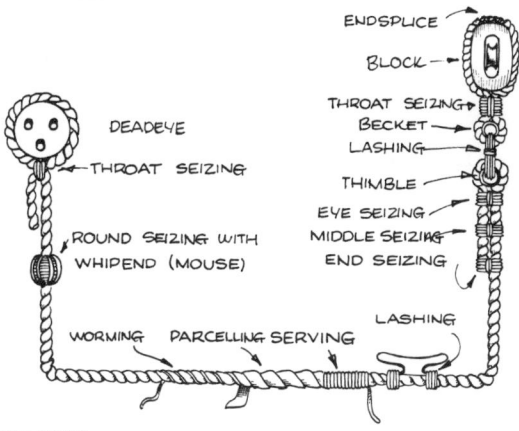

Fig. 98. Rope ways

Serving is winding spun yarn tightly about the rope.

Parceling is bandaging the rope with small narrow strips of tarred canvas.

Mast Shrouds and Stays

Shrouds. The shrouds (10-1/2-in. fore and main and 6-1/2-in. mizzen) are the lateral supports of the mast and were wormed, parceled, and served. As I could not obtain hawser type rope (some of the large surgical silk is braided and does not imitate the appearance of large hemp rope), I utilized twisted nylon fish line, which when dyed black, works very well. In securing a rope to the end of a deadeye, I recommend an absolute pearl—I used a standard surgical hemostat to hold the ropes together while applying a throat or eye seize. Most of the deadeyes were throat seized on the large vessel, however, on the model eye seizing is perfectly satisfactory. The hemostat will hold the rope in place while the seizing is done and lightly glued, thus firmly holding the shroud in position on the deadeye as noted in Fig. 99. This method will save many hours of frustration in attempts to hold the shroud without slipping off the deadeyes. For the lanyards #2-0 silk was used (5-in. circumference). A double end knot (the Matthew Walker knot) was used on the fixed end, lightly touched with glue, and then passed or reeved through the subsequent and successive deadeye holes and

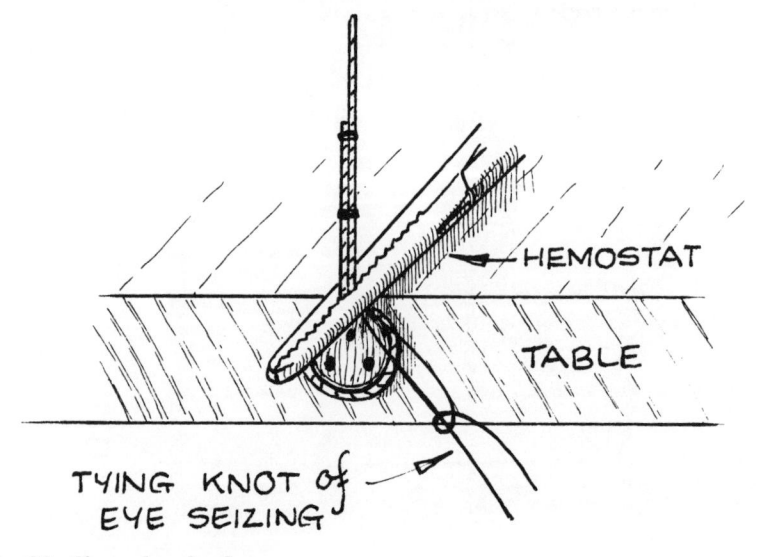

Fig. 99. Shroud to deadeye

STANDING RIGGING 111

secured finally around the aforementioned eye seizing with double half hitch. This is bulky but was the standard method employed as noted in Fig. 100. My second pearl is to place a touch of glue on the end of each lanyard or any other piece of rigging to be reeved through a block or deadeye. This is accomplished by placing a touch of model airplane cement or glue on the end of the rope and wiping it off in a twisting fashion, thus stiffening and tapering the rope so that it will readily pass through the drilled holes in blocks or deadeyes. (The area through which a rope is reeved in a block is called the swallow.) I might mention here several advantages to utilizing some small surgical tools to facilitate the intricate job of rigging the model. A pair of bayonet or

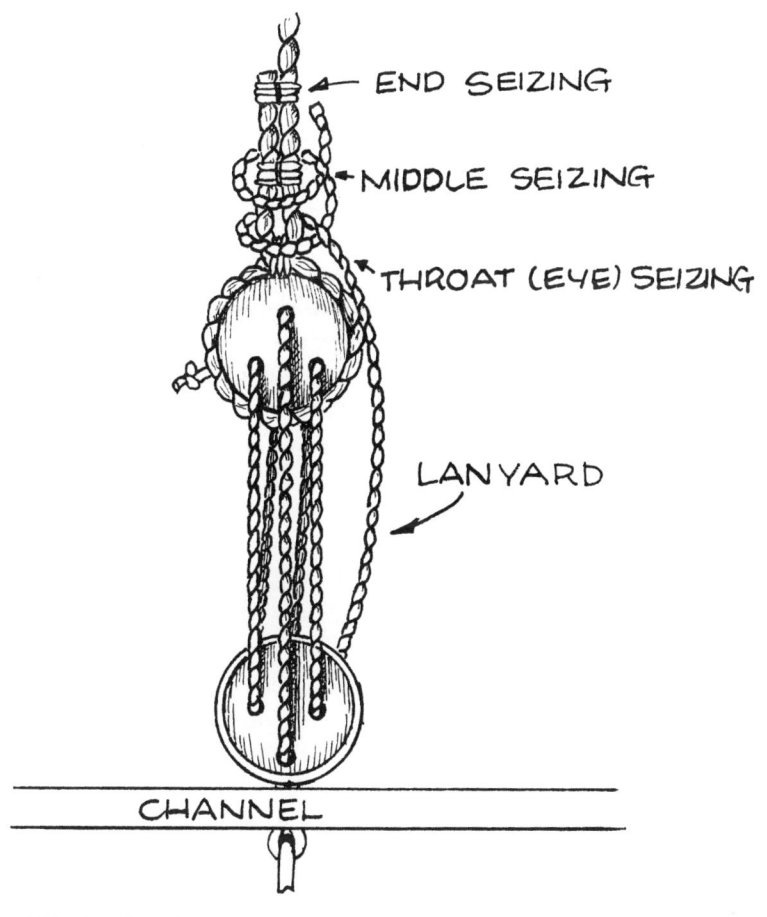

Fig. 100. Deadeye lanyard

bent nasal packing forceps is excellent for picking up small items. Straight and curved hemostats (mosquito, small Kelly, or Crile) are excellent tools for holding rigging in place while seizing, serving, or securing. Ring forceps and long straight and curved forceps are a great help in picking up pieces of debris or small fittings especially those that fall in the depths of the model. Also a great help is to learn to tie a one-hand surgical knot. This is noted in Fig. 101, courtesy Ethicon. Tying one-handed knots on a large rigged ship model may literally save hours in knot tying and is fairly easy to learn.

The first of each lower shroud is called a "swifter" and is constructed of two triple blocks instead of the deadeyes. The standing purchase is a stropped triple block, secured to the channel, as are the deadeyes, with brass chains and chain plate. The lanyard or free end is then secured on a cleat lashed to the shroud or to an eyebolt secured into the channel. It may be of interest while discussing the shrouds to include a view of the way shrouds were set up on the full-sized vessel (from Polland) using a masthead pendant attached to a tackle fixed to a shroud as shown in Fig. 102.

Each shroud was secured to its deadeye and lanyard. Then it was taken over the bolster about the masthead and eye seized to pass back down again to the channel to be seized to the next deadeye. This process was repeated for each successive shroud alternating port and starboard at the masthead to maintain an equal lateral mast tension or balance. The respective sizes of the deadeyes were 3/8-in. main, 5/16-in. fore, and 1/4-in. mizzen and constructed in a method noted previously (Fig. 83). It should be noted that at the completion of each shroud, the angled deadeye support chains and chain plates were drilled and nailed in place in a contiguous line to maintain a pleasing appearance. A method shown in Fig. 103 to keep the lineup of deadeyes parallel with the waterline and not the plank sheer is to place a small piece of wood cut to the proper height and size and placed on the deck frames behind the deadeyes enabling one to sight the position of the deadeyes laterally and make it parallel with the horizon or waterline. It takes a little time to make but saves time as the shroud placement proceeds.

Ratlines. The original ratlines were 1-1/2 in. circumference. Those for the model were made from #3-0 black silk, round seized and then clove hitched between each shroud as shown (Fig. 103). The first ratline was really a wire or iron batten (0.031 in.), seized about each

STANDING RIGGING 113

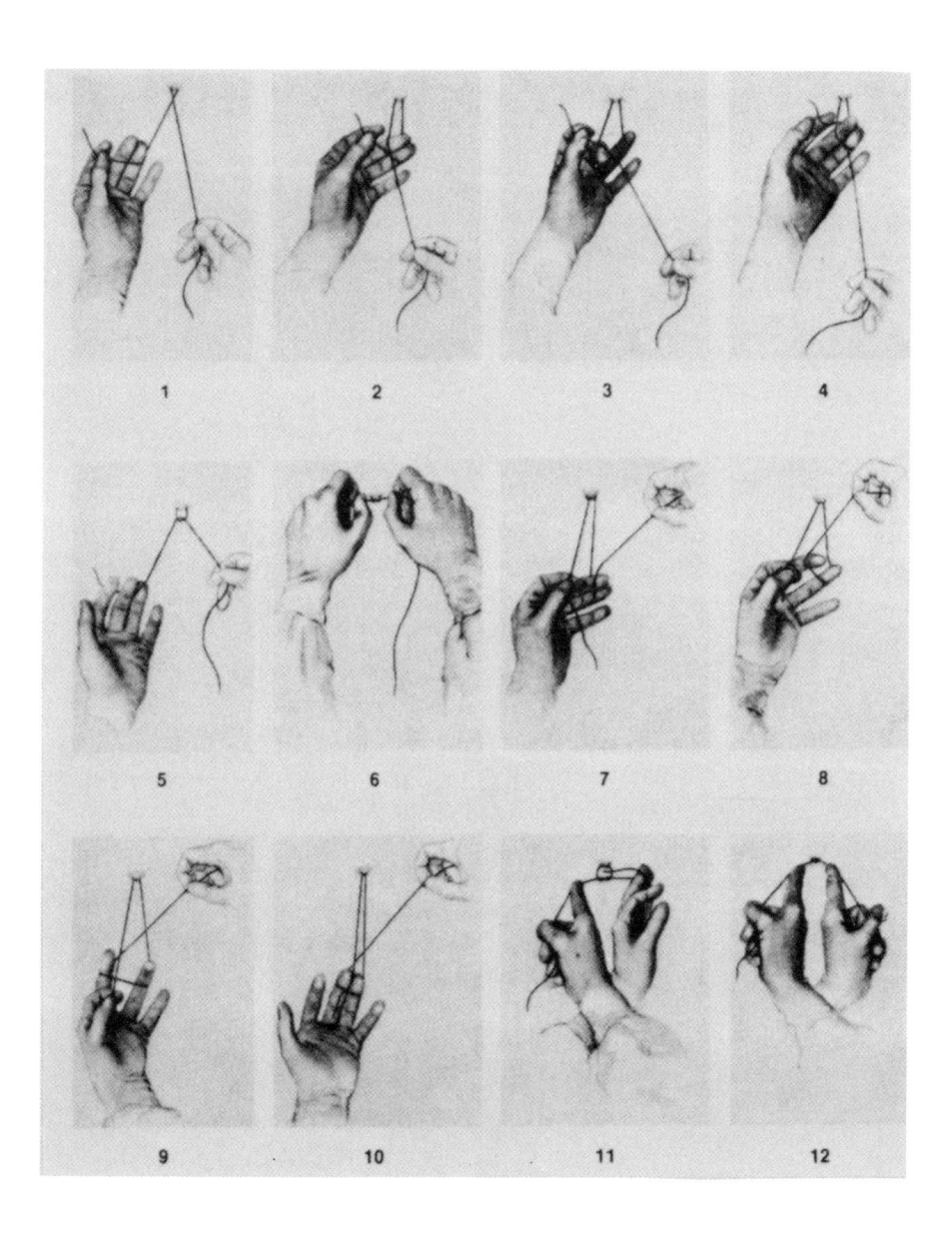

NOTE: Shown here is the left hand beginning the knot with the short end of the ligature. However, either hand may be used with this initial step.

Fig. 101. "One hand tie": Courtesy Ethicon Corporation from *Manual of Operative Procedures*

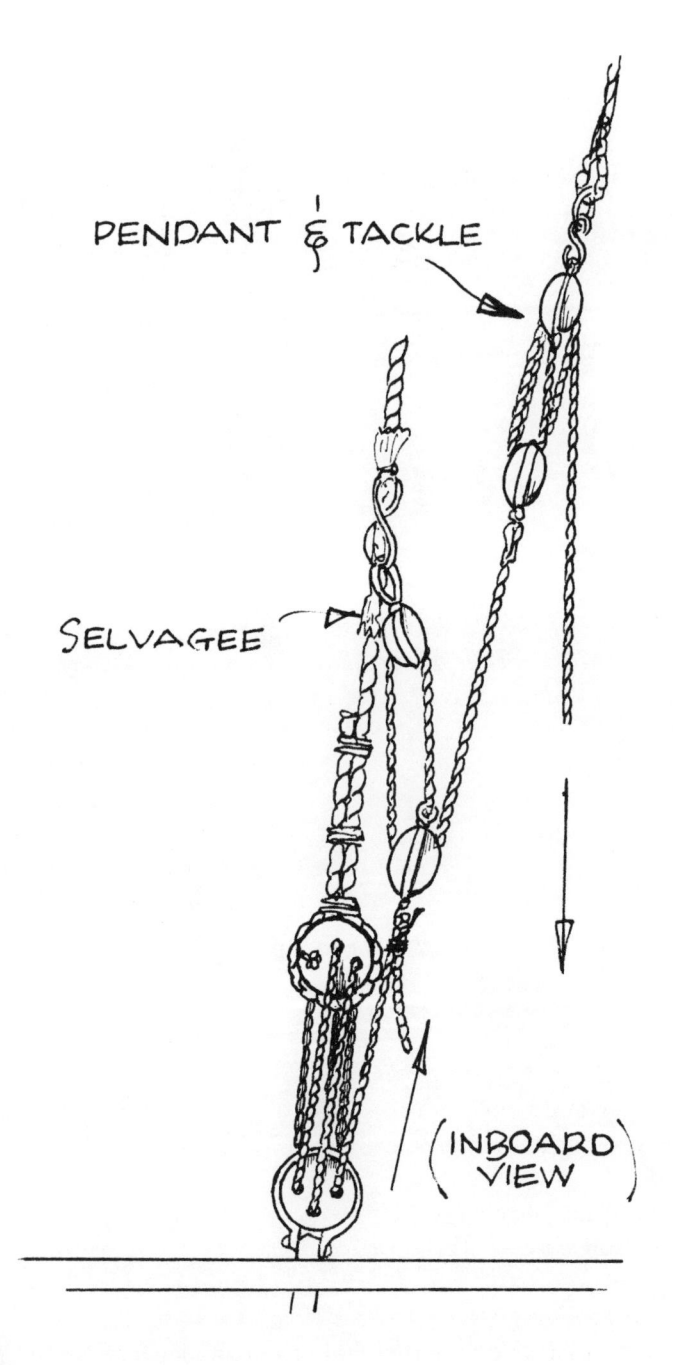

Fig. 102. Setting up shrouds

STANDING RIGGING 115

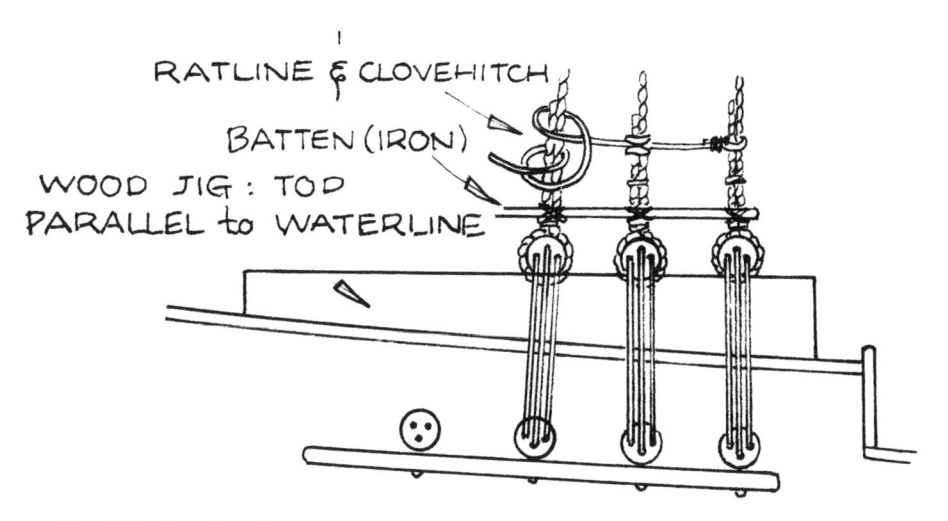

Fig. 103. Deadeye jig

shroud at the position of the eye seizing on the deadeye. The distance separating the ratlines was approximately 1/4 in. to correspond to the 1 ft or 14-in. distance between ratlines on a regular vessel. Topmast deadeyes of 1/8-in. cherry wood were placed through the previously drilled holes in the mast top. These deadeyes had been stropped with 3/8-in. cut brass rings and then inserted through square holes in the mast top. (These drill holes were squared off with square needle files to facilitate the strop's placement as explained with reference to main channels in Chapter IV.

Bentinck Shrouds. Once the topmast deadeyes were in place, the mast top futtock shrouds, which were made for #2-0 silk, were seized to the deadeye strops. Then they were taken down to the main shrouds where they were lashed to an oaken or metal batten (0.031 wire on the model), and seized to a thimble which was secondarily secured to a Bentinck shroud which in turn was purchased to a deadeye and lanyard on the deck inboard near the fore belaying pin rack as shown in Fig. 104.

Catharpins. Secured to the battens as is noted (Fig. 104), catharpins were made of #2-0 silk (6 in. circumference).

Pendants. Two large, 11-in. ropes were placed over each masthead with an eye at one end and a thimble at the other. These hung down 16 to 20 feet below the masthead and were handy for use as pendants for the securing of tackles and blocks to cinch up shrouds and

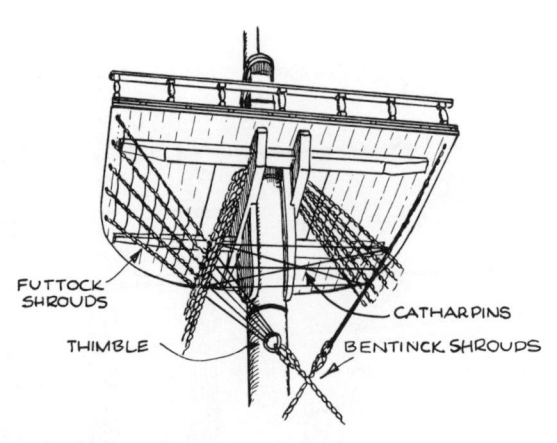

Fig. 104. Bentinck shrouds

to assist hoisting yards, sail gear, and spars or swaying up a top mast, etc. On the model they were made of #5 silk, 3/64 in. diameter and lashed to the masthead near the bolsters.

Topmast shrouds. Prepared like the lower main shrouds, the topmast shrouds used (main and fore 6 in., mizzen 4-1/2 in.) 1/8-in. deadeyes and #3-0 black silk for lanyards and ratlines. Fig. 105 demonstrates the maintop relationship with main yard; Fig. 106 is a view of the main topmast crosstrees. The fore and main lower shrouds were eight in number with respect to large deadeyes while the mizzen had five.

Backstays. The main and fore-topmast had two backstays, each standing 6-1/2 in. made up of #1-0 silk. They were turned to 1/8-in. deadeyes at the channels and seized at the top masthead. Each mast also has a topgallant backstay (4 in.) secured to the channel with a deadeye and turned and served at the appropriate mast junction made up of 0-black silk. Each mast also has a royal backstay (3 in.) turned and seized at the royal topmast and to the most aft 1/8-in. deadeye of each channel. Neither topgallant nor royal backstay deadeyes were secured by chain plates but merely bolted to the channels.

Topgallant Shrouds. Instead of the usual attachment to eyebolts secured in a mast band below the trestletrees, the topgallant shrouds (3-1/2 in.) were turned and served on a common thimble which in turn was secured to a Bentinck type shroud attached to a 1/8-in. deadeye, the lower one of which was stropped to an eyebolt in the mainmast top planking. There were no deadeyes nor ratlines on the topgallant

STANDING RIGGING 117

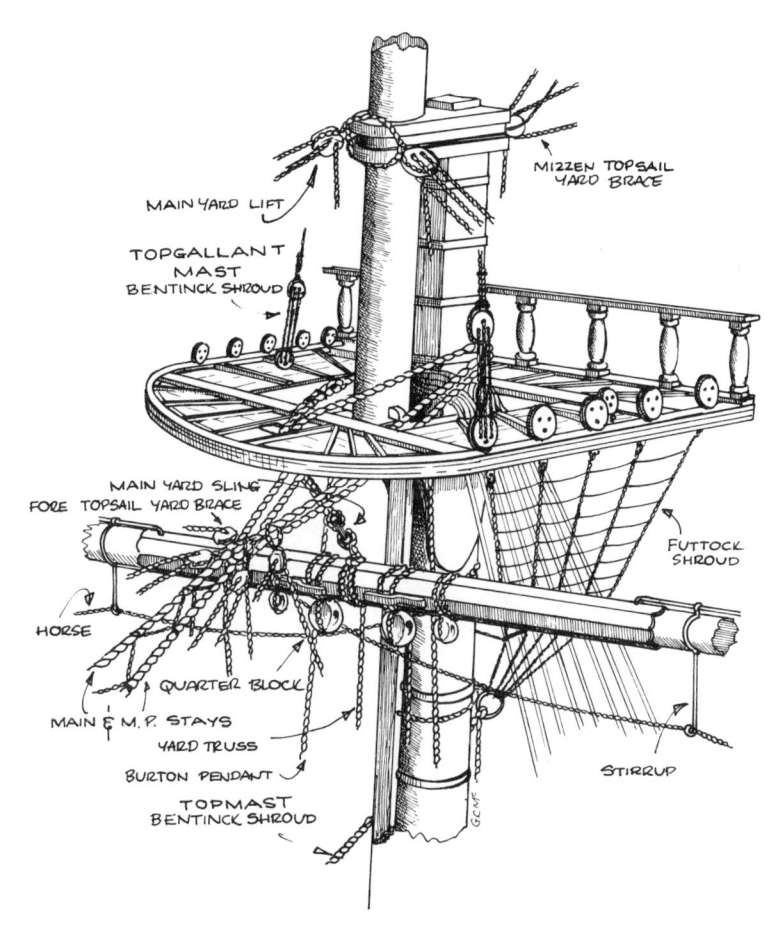

Fig. 105. Main top

shrouds. Instead, access to the royal mast and yards was via a Jacob's ladder. This ladder was constructed of two stays (#2-0 silk) secured to eyebolts in the aft part of the trestletrees and secured to the masthead of the topgallant mast where the ropes of Jacob's ladder were served. Ratlines on the Jacob's ladder were made of #3-0 black silk. The futtock shrouds, topgallant shrouds, and Jacob's ladder are shown in Fig. 106.

Mainstay and Main Preventer Stay. These were the largest and the most important stays of the ship (17-1/2 in. and 12 in., respectively). They were secured over the main masthead and in a sling or eye about the masthead and retained with a mouse. They may be made of

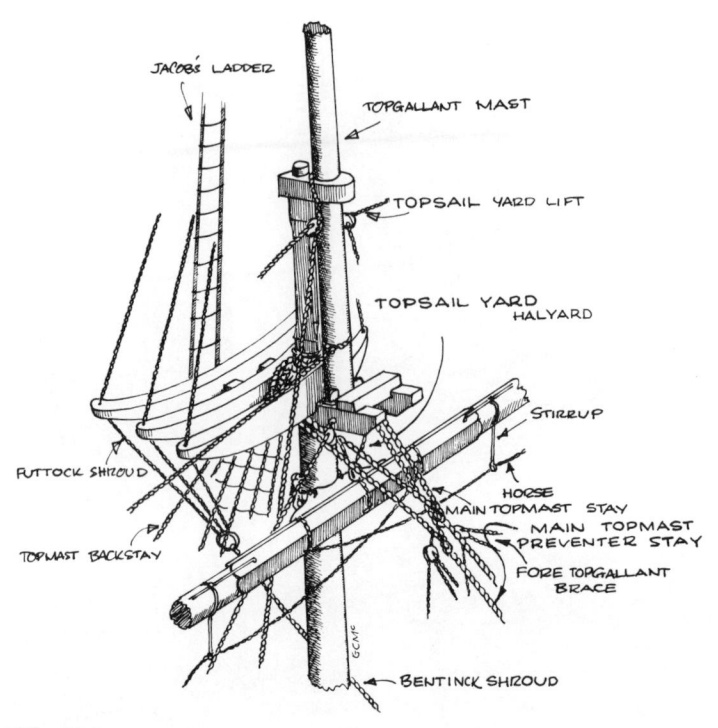

Fig. 106. Main topmast

1/16-in. black dyed nylon which mimics cable-laid rope. The slings were eye seized in front of the mouse, with middle and end seizing to secure the pulling attachment, as shown in Fig. 107. The mainstay and main preventer stay then passed port and starboard of the foremast to be turned over hearteyes. Hearteyes are large deadeyes, the center section of which is a singular, triangular hole instead of the standard three holes in a deadeye. The lanyard for the hearteyes were made from #2-0 silk with approximately 10 turns and then half hitched over the next hearteye seizing. Lower hearteyes were secured by strop and eyebolts to either side of the bow bulwark companionway. These two mainstays were snaked together with #3-0 silk (Fig. 107). The apparent reason for snaking the two stays together was that if one was split with cannon-shot or by other means during battle, the other stay could be supported by the snake rope and more readily repaired.

Forestays and Fore Preventer Stay. The main forestay (1/16 in.) was also made of 1/16-in., four-strand, cable-laid rope with mouse and

STANDING RIGGING

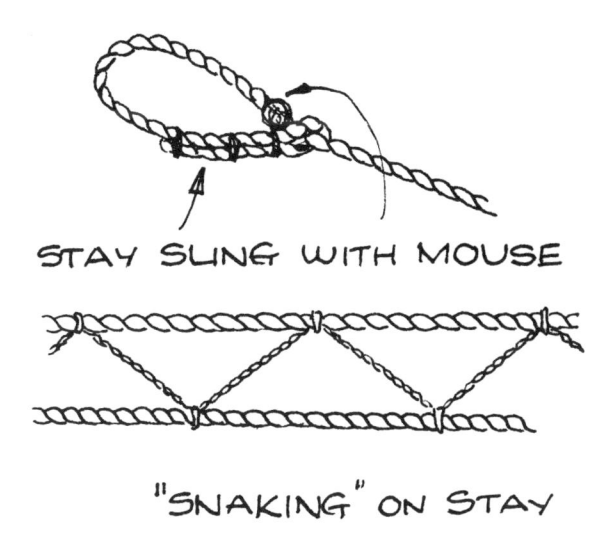

Fig. 107. Stay sling, mouse, and snaking

triple seized sling secured to the foremasthead. The main preventer stay (10-1/2 in.) was made of #2-0 silk. Open hearteyes were also employed with large open hearts collared to the bowsprit cheeks as noted in Fig. 108, and were constructed of 1/4-in. thick and 1-in. wide and 1-1/4-in. long cherry stock, grooved to fit over the jibboom and lashed in place with #1-0 silk to the bowsprit utilizing retaining grooves cut in the bowsprit cheeks. The two forestays and fore preventer stays were also snaked with #3-0 black silk.

Mizzen Stay. The upper end arranged with sling and mouse as were the other stays, the mizzen stay (8 in.), made from #2 silk, subsequently passed through a bull's-eye seized on a collar which passed about the mainmast with one end through the rubbing paunch.

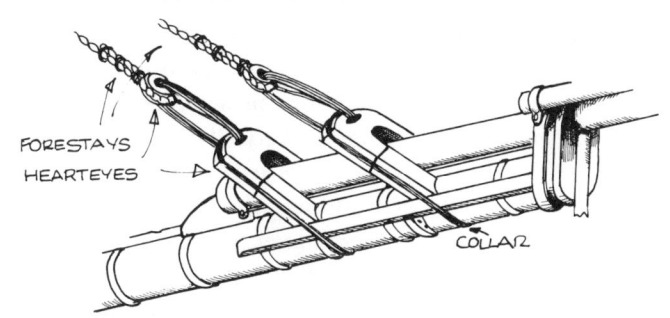

Fig. 108. Forestays and hearteyes

The collar was lashed to the mast as noted in Fig. 109. The lower end of the stay was seized on a bight to a bull's-eye stropped to an eyebolt in the deck near the mainmast foot.

Main-Topmast Preventer Stays. For the main-topmast preventer stays (6 in.), I used #1 silk. The topmast end was attached similar to other stays (also, at this point, it may be well to mention that a knot in the rope may serve just as well as the mouse to prevent the sling from overriding the rope). This stay subsequently reeved through a bull's-eye seized on a bight of a collar lashed below the main cheeks and hence to be set up as a lanyard turned and seized to an eyebolt on the deck near the foremast foot on the starboard side.

Main-Topmast Stay. For this stay (7-1/2 in.), I used #1 silk. One end was secured over the top masthead, seized with mouse and sling, then reeved through a single block seized on a collar lashed about the masthead above the main shroud at the level of the fore top trestletrees. It was then set up seized on a thimble hooked on a ring eyebolt near the foremast foot.

Mizzen Topmast Stay. For the mizzen topmast stay (4-1/2 in.), I employed #1 silk. The upper end was secured and seized with mouse and sling. The stay was reeved through a 3/32-in. single block, stropped, and seized to a collar at the level of the main shrouds, and then reeved again through a bull's-eye seized or stropped to an eyebolt, starboard side, mainmast foot.

Mizzen Topgallant Stay. I used #0 silk begun as loop and eye at the topgallant mast junction. It was reeved through a 3/32-in. block stropped to an eyebolt epoxied into the mainmast cap, and subsequently seized to a thimble in an eyebolt on the port side of the mainmast foot. (The original stay was 3-1/2 in. circumference.)

Mizzen Royal Stay. I used #0 silk. The upper end was secured as eye and mouse at royal mast, then reeved through a thimble collared at the level of the main-topmast shrouds or main-topmast trestletrees. Then it was brought down the mast to be seized on a thimble in an eyebolt near the mainmast foot. Parenthetically, it should be noted that although the order of the stays as presented appears random, it is not. By rigging the stays in this order (doing the lower stays first) all stays tend to keep taut since the upper mizzen stays, and proceeding forward to the main, foremast, and finally the bowsprit stays, tend to pull forward and leave the lower stays fairly well undisturbed. (The original was 3 in. circumference.)

STANDING RIGGING 121

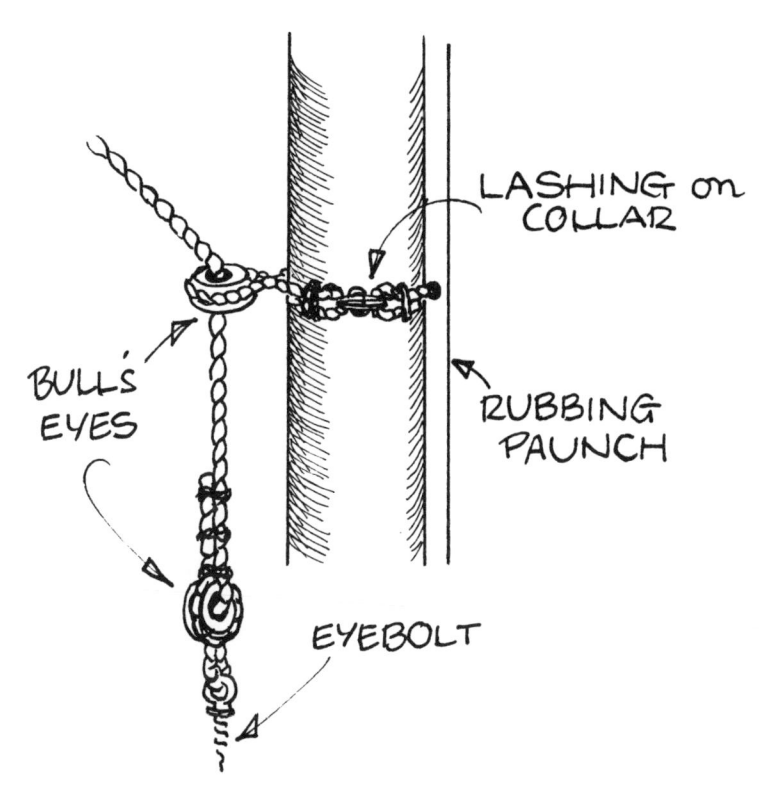

Fig. 109. Mizzen stay

Main-Topgallant Stay. I used #1 silk begun as eye and loop at main-topgallant masthead, subsequently reeved through a 3/32-in. block which was stropped and seized to a collar about the foremast at the level of the foremast trestletrees. It was then seized in a bull's-eye and stropped to a deck eyebolt on the aft port side of the foremast foot. (The original was 4 in. circumference.)

Main Royal Stay. I used #0 silk begun as eye and loop at the royal masthead, reeved through a 1/16-in. block which was stropped to an eyebolt and expoxied in the topgallant mast cap. Then it was seized to a thimble hooked to an eyebolt in the deck near the aft starboard side of the foremast foot. (The original was 3 in. circumference.)

Bowsprit Supports and Stays

Gammoning. Gammoning was used to lash the bowsprit in place to the stem. I used #2 black silk or 3/64 in. diameter black rope which was wrapped ten turns about the bowsprit and reeved through the gammoning hole in the stempiece. Several cross turns were made and the ends lashed together. (The original gammoning was 8 in. circumference.)

Bob Stays. I used #2 silk for the bob stays, three which were seized through three 1/16-in. holes drilled in the stempiece. They were then seized to a bull's-eye with its lanyard of #2-0 silk to another stropped bull's eye, collared to the lower bowsprit, supported with small wooden stop cleats. (The original stays were 8 in. circumference.)

Bowsprit Shrouds. I used #2-0 silk for the bowsprit shrouds which were secured by seizing an eyebolt positioned midway in the white stripe forward of the first gunport. Then they were secured by seizing them to a bull's-eye with #2-0 silk lanyard stropped to an eyebolt in the bowsprit cheek, 1/4 in. aft of the bowsprit cap. (The original shrouds were 8 in. circumference.)

Fore-topmast Stay. I used #2 silk begun as loop and eye at the fore-topmast trestletree, then reeved through small sheaves, positioned in the starboard fore part of the bowsprit cheek, 1/8 in. aft of the bowsprit cap. Subsequently it was seized on a becket to a 3/16 in., stropped, double block connected by its fall (#2-0 silk) to a single block, and finally stropped to an eyebolt secured in the planking, 1/4 in. to the junction of the head rail and its ekeing. The end of the fall was belayed to the largest timberhead near the cathead. (The original was 7-1/2 in. circumference.)

Fore-Topmast Preventer Stay. I used #1 silk. The stay was made identical in run to that of the foremast stay except it was smaller and was reeved through the port bowsprit cheek with the same luff tackle and fall securement to the large bow port timberhead, as shown in Fig. 110. (The original was 5-1/2 in. circumference.)

Jib Stay. I used #0 silk. The jib stay was begun seized to the jibboom, 1 in. aft of the flying jibboom cap, hence to a 3/32-in. block, stropped, and seized to a collar at the fore-topmast trestletrees, then through the fore top lubber's hole to be seized on a thimble, and secured to an eyebolt in the deck aft of the port side foremast foot (Fig. 110). (The original was 5 in. circumference.)

Fore-Topgallant Stay. I used #0 silk begun as eye and mouse topgallant top, reeved through the middle of a triple thimble to port side, therefore through a small fairlead beneath the bowsprit cheeks to be seized to a bull's-eye, and stropped with wire to an eyebolt near the base of the bowsprit. (The original was 4-in. circumference.)

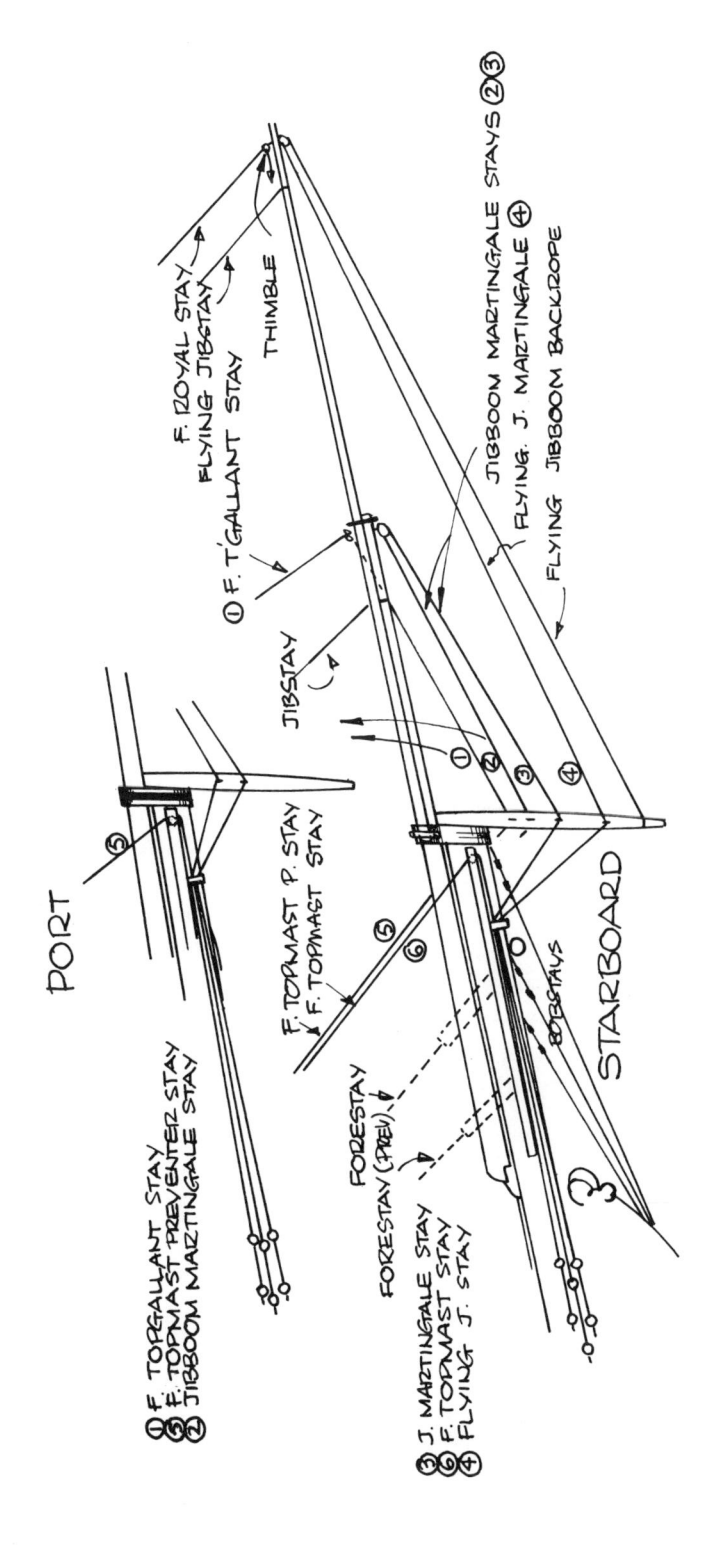

Fig. 110. Stays to bowsprit

Flying Jib Stay. I used #0 silk. The flying jib stay was begun next to the topgallant stay, then reeved through a thimble seized in a collar, 3/16 in. from the end of the flying jibboom to starboard to belay on the second belaying pin and the bow bulwark starboard pin rail. (The original was 2-1/2 in. circumference.)

Fore Royal Stay. I used #0 silk. The fore royal stay was begun as eye and mouse at the fore royal mast, was reeved through a thimble collared 5/8 in. aft of the flying jibboom top, then brought to port to belay to the second belaying pin of the starboard bow pin rack. (The original was 2-1/2 in. circumference.)

Martingales. The *flying jibboom martingale* was seized on a lower dolphin striker eyebolt, then reeved through a 3/32-in. block, stropped and collared to the flying jibboom tip, then back under a lower dolphin striker fairlead, then reeved through a hole in the accessory transverse bowsprit cheek, and then set up starboard in the same manner as the fore topgallant stay with two bull's-eyes and a #3-0 silk lanyard. (The original was 5 in. circumference.)

Jibboom martingales were originally seized to a stropped bull's-eye anchored to a port eyebolt as the base of the bowsprit with a #3-0 silk lanyard seized to a bull's-eye. The stay was then reeved through the port accessory bowsprit cheek fairlead and port dolphin striker to be reeved through a 3/32-in. single block collared to the head of the jibboom. The martingale passed back through a fairlead on the starboard of the dolphin striker, though the accessory bowsprit cheek fairlead to be setup with bull's-eyes identical to its aforementioned origin near the flying jibboom martingale at the base of the bowsprit. The position of these stays is noted in Fig. 110. The jibboom shrouds or stays are noted after discussion of the construction of the spritsail yard as they were reeved through eyebolts on this yard.

CHAPTER VI
Running Rigging

The easiest way to describe the running rigging is to describe it for each yard and mast. Since many of the yards are rigged similarly, I will avoid unnecessary repetition where possible.

The best rigging line to use is white linen which has been dyed with tea or similar substance to imitate hemp. The major reason for using it is that it does not fray like cotton, is very durable, and is more resistant to variations in temperature.

Jackstays and Horses

The jackstays and horses were previously described under the discussion of yard assembly (Chapter IV.). Stirrups were made of small brass wires wrapped around the yard with a small end loop to hold the horse ropes. The horses were similar for all yards excluding the occasional use of a Flemish horse which is a loop from the outside stirrup to an eyebolt in the end of the yardarm. Sheets, tacks, clew lines, buntlines, bowlines, leech lines and their attendant blocks are not discussed at length as there are no sails on the model. (The originals were jackstay 3-1/2 in. and horse 4 in. circumference respectively.)

Foremast

Lower Foreyard Sling. The yard slings are as noted in illustration of the main yard (Fig. 95). The originals were 12 to 14 in. circumference and 1/16-in. black silk was utilized in the model. One end had an eye splice in it. This end would go down through the hole in the mast top over a small bolster and was seized on a bite with a thimble (the thimble could be left off on the small models and only a little loop or becket is needed). The other end of the sling then was passed back up through the mast top, around the masthead and reeved through itself with the end eye splice and triply seized. A second piece of rope which was the yard section of the sling was looped on itself around the yard, seized as a bite on another thimble which was in turn lashed with a lanyard to the initial or first thimble part of the sling, thus completing the sling. If this description seems complex or long, I recommend glancing at the illustration of the sling (Fig. 95) which will simplify it.

Truss. Two ropes of #2 black silk were utilized with thimbles seized on the ends of each. On the mast side of each yard, the thimbled ends were throat seized on themselves and after each rope had been passed around the mast, the starboard end pendant was reeved through the port thimble and vice versa. As the rope neared the deck, each end was seized or turned on a 1/4-in. double block attached by its #3-0 silk fall to another 1/4-in. single block secured to an eyebolt in the deck near the mast foot. The fall of each luff tackle was then belayed on a cleat on the inner surface of the foremast bitts as noted in Fig. 111. (The original was 9 in. circumference.)

Lifts. For lifts 1/4-in. double blocks (15 in.) were stropped and seized in ropes looped about the junction of the top mast and the foretop mast cap. These bitts were buttressed by a rope with a loop seized on each end and looped below and forward of the mast cap. A 1/4-in. (15 in.) single block was seized on a short segment of a rope and secured to the yard and yardarm junction. For the lift #2-0 linen was seized on a becket of the single block, reeved through the double block, back through the single block, hence again reeved through the double block, down the sides of the masthead through the lubber's hole to

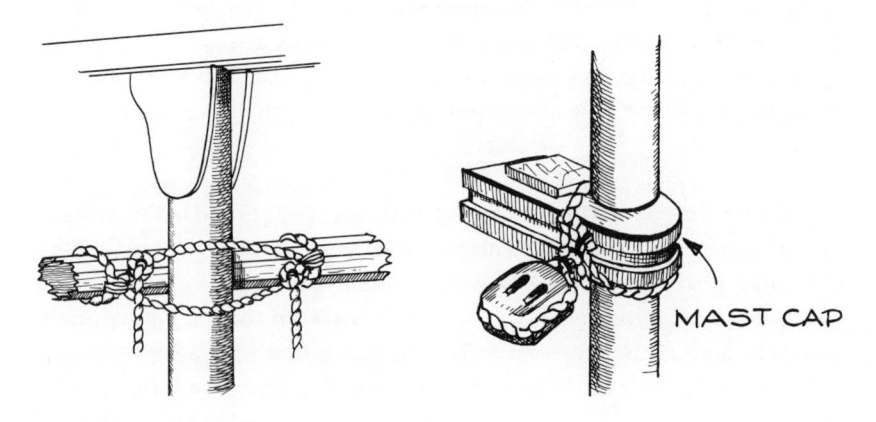

Fig. 111. Truss pendant

Fig. 112. Yard lift block

belay on the side pin racks of the foremast as shown in Fig. 112. (The original was 5 in. circumference.)

Braces. A 1/4-in. single block (15-in.) was seized on a short length of rope, #1 linen, the end of which had been turned and seized on the yardarm. The brace (4 in.), #3-0 linen rope, was turned and seized on the sling of the mainstay, reeved through the single yardarm block, and then reeved through a second block, also collared and seized on the mainstay. Then it was brought down along the mainstay to be reeved finally through another 1/4-in. block attached to the lower mainstay near the foremast, and subsequently belayed on the foremast lateral pin rack.

Fore Topsail Yard

Truss. The yard was kept in place on the mast with a parral attached to the wooden truss eyebolts as noted (Fig. 96). The trucks were 3/32-in. black Indian beads; the ribs were 1/32-in. oak shim pieces cut to fit.

Lift. I used #2-0 linen. The standing part was seized on a collar lashed about the topgallant mast, midway between the crosstrees and topmast cap, then reeved through a single block seized to the yardarm, subsequently reeved through another 1/8-in. single block seized on a collar about the topmast cap, hence to be belayed on the pin rack on both sides of the foremast. (The original was 3-1/2 in. circumference.)

Halyard. Two 1/8-in. single blocks were stropped and eyebolted to the undersurface of each topmast trestletree near the mast. A 1/8-in. block was seized and secured to the topsail yard with a seized and lashed collar about the midpoint of this yard. The halyard (4 in.), #2-0 line, was reeved through each of these single blocks as noted in Fig. 1☆. Then each end was passed port and starboard to be seized into a 1/8-in. double block which was, in turn, attached by a luff tackle fall to a 1/8-in. single block stropped to an eyebolt in the fore channel, port and starboard, which subsequently was belayed to a cleat lashed to the second fore shroud or to the side belaying pin rack.

Braces. I used #2-0 linen. Braces were begun collared and seized on the sling of the topmast stay, subsequently reeved through a 1/8-in. block, stropped and seized in a rope secured to the yardarm junction of the topsail yard. Then they were reeved through a 3/16-in. single block, seized and secured to a collar lashed to the main stay sling to end belayed to the mainmast fife rail. (The original was 3-1/2 in. circumference.)

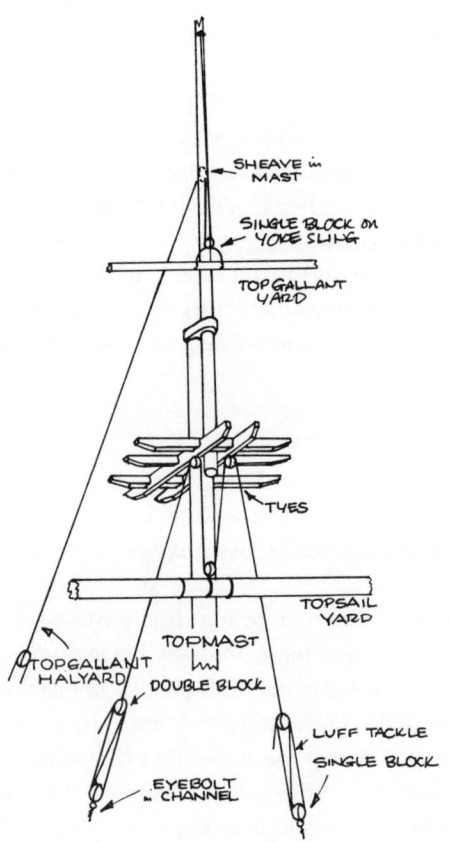

Fig. 1☆. Halyards

Fore Topgallant Yard

Truss. This was a smaller parral made with small 1/16-in. black Indian beads with very small ribs made from 1/64-in. sheet plastic painted black. There are no slings.

Lifts. I used #2-0 linen. The standing end was seized on a thimble, and seized and collared at the top masthead below the royal pole. It then reeved through 3/32-in. block seized and stropped to a rope at the topgallant yardarm, and through a 3/32-in. block seized and collared to the royal pole above the top masthead. Finally, it passes down along the side of the mast to be belayed on the foremast fife rail. (The original was 3 in. circumference.)

Halyard. I used #2-0 linen (Fig. 1☆). The halyard was begun secured or seized on a bitt at the heading of the royal pole and reeved through a 1/32-in. single wood block seized on the loop or becket of a rope collared around the midline of the topgallant yard. Then it was reeved through a sheave in the royal mast pole to descend on the starboard side to be seized on a 1/8-in. double block, the fall of which was attached to a single block to be subsequently belayed to the starboard pin rack. The single block was stropped and eyebolted to the starboard channel. (The original was 3 in. circumference.)

Braces. I used #2-0 linen. The braces were begun seized to the main topmast stay sling, reeved through a 3/32-in. block at the yardarm, then reeved to another block, seized, and collared at the main topmast sling. Finally they reeved through a 3/32-in. block stropped to a lashed collar at the fore masthead to be belayed in the foremast fife rail. (The original was 3 in. circumference.)

Fore Royal Yard

Truss. A parral with small beads. The only slings are those from the lower yards; all the rest of the yards are positioned on the mast with parrals of varying sizes. (The original was 3 in. circumference.)

Lifts. I used #2-0 linen. These were seized on a yardarm (or 1/16-in. single block, stropped, and collared at same level) and reeved through sheaves in the heading of the royal mast. They were then brought down along the mast to be belayed on the foremast fife rail. (The original was 3 in. circumference.)

Halyard. I used #2-0 linen. The halyard was seized to the midsection yard, reeved through a sheave in the royal mast, then brought down on the port side to be turned and seized on a 3/32-in. double block which was tackled to a stropped, single block secured to the port foremast channel on an eyebolt. The fall was belayed to the port pin rack. (The original was 3 in. circumference.)

Braces. I used #3-0 linen. They were seized on the yardarm and each was reeved through a small double block, stropped and collared to the heading of the main royal mast and then brought down on either side of the mast to belayed in the main fife rail. (The original was 2 in. circumference.)

Mainmast Yard

Mainyard. Sling, lifts, and truss are identical to the foremast yard including belaying the fall of the truss pendants, to cleats on the inside of the mainmast bitts.

Braces. I used #2-0 linen. A large, 5/16-in. single block was seized to a rope which had been secured and eye seized to the yardarm junction. This block was reeved by a brace, the standing end of which had been seized on a becket from a 5/16-in. single block previously seized on a collar on the quarter gallery main brace bumpkin. The fall was then reeved through this bumpkin block and subsequently reeved through a sheave in the bulwark near the aft spar deck gunport to be cleated on the inner bulwark cleat near the aft side of this gunport—same port and starboard. (The original was 4 in. circumference.)

Main Topsail Yard

Halyard. Parrals, lifts and halyards are the same, as for the foremast yard. The fall from the halyard luff tackle was also belayed on the port and starboard bulwark pin racks.

Braces. I used #2-0 linen. These were begun seized on a collar on the mizzen topmast stay sling, reeved through a 3/16-in. single block at yardarm, and then reeved through a 3/16-in. single block collared on the sling of the mizzen stay to be belayed on the side bulwark pin rack. (The original was 3-1/2 in. circumference.)

Main Topgallant Yard

The parral and lifts are same as the topgallant yard. The halyard to luff tackle was secured in the mainmast starboard channels with the fall to the main bulwark pin rack.

Braces. I used #2-0 linen. The braces were begun seized in the mizzenmast topmast stay, reeved through a 1/8-in. block attached to the yardarm, reeved back though a 1/8-in. block seized and collared on the same mizzenmast topmast stay, and then brought down to the mast and belayed on the mizzenmast pin rack. (The original was 2-1/2 in. circumference.)

Royal Yard

The parral, lift, and halyard were the same as the halyard to the port main channel. The topgallant yard, it will be recalled, had a starboard luff tackle consistently.

Braces. I used #3-0 linen. The braces were seized at the yardarm, reeved through a small 3/32-in. block collared on the heading of the mizzen royal mast, and brought down along the mast to end belayed to the mizzenmast pin rack. (The original was 2 in. circumference.)

RUNNING RIGGING

Mizzenmast Yard

Crossjack or Loweryard. Although years before the construction of the *Constellation*, the lateen rigged mizzen yard had disappeared from common usage the name crossjack persisted. It literally crossed the mizzenmast fore and aft and was utilized as a large jib sail like the Arab dhows of today or the Barbary pirate feluccas of the Mediterranean several centuries ago. At any rate, the mizzen main yard was rigged similarly to the lower yards of the other masts with the exception of smaller ropes and thimbles.

Slings. I used #3-0 linen. The standing end of the brace was seized to a becket, stropped to a 1/8-in. double block seized on the bitt of a collar lashed about the mainmast at the lower end of the mainmast cheeks. It was then belayed to the mainmast fife rails. An alternative route of the mizzen brace could be reeved through a single block, seized and collared to the futtock shroud and main shroud junction batten and then belayed to the bulwark pin rack. (The original slings were 10 in. circumference; the lifts were 3 in. circumference.)

Mizzen Topsail Yard

The parral and lift were unchanged. I used #3-0 linen. The lift was reeved through a 1/8-in. block, seized and collared to the mizzen topmast head, and then belayed in the mizzen pin rack. The halyard was the same as the purchase of the luff tackle on the starboard mizzen channel. For the brace I also used #3-0 linen. The standing end of the brace was seized on a becket to a 1/8-in. double block, stropped to an eyebolt, secured with epoxy to the mainmast cap, reeved through a 1/8-in. seized yardarm block, and then brought back through the aforementioned mainmast cap double block to be belayed on the main fife rail. (The original lift was 3 in. circumference; the brace 4-1/2 in. circumference.)

Mizzen Top Gallant Yard

Parral, lift, and halyard were the same as fore topgallant yard, luff tackle purchasing to starboard side and channel with #3-0 linen suture serving as its fall.

Lifts. These were different from the fore and mainmast in that there were no yardarm blocks. They were merely seized at the yardarm, reeved through a 1/8-in. block, seized on a collar at the royal masthead, and then belayed to the bulwark pin rack.

Braces. I used #3-0 linen. The standing end was seized on a becket to a 1/16-in. single block, stropped and eyebolted to the aft main topmast trestletrees. The fall was belayed to the main fife rails. (The original was 1-1/2 in. circumference.)

Mizzen Royal Yards

The parral, lift, and halyard were unchanged, with the halyard fall to the luff tackle at the port mizzen channel. I used #3-0 linen for the braces which were seized at the yardarm, reeved through a 1/8-in. single block, stropped to eyebolts secured in the medial aft main topmast trestletrees, with fall belayed to the mainmast fife rail. (The original brace was 1 in. circumference.)

Spanker Gaff

Parral. The parral utilized no ribs but instead small 3/64-in. or 1/6-in. black Indian beads, seized on eyebolts at the gaff jaws.

Peak halyard. I used #2-0 linen. See Fig. 114. The peak halyard was begun seized on the aft end of the gaff, reeved through a 1/4-in. triple block, stropped to an eyebolt, and secured or epoxied into the aft

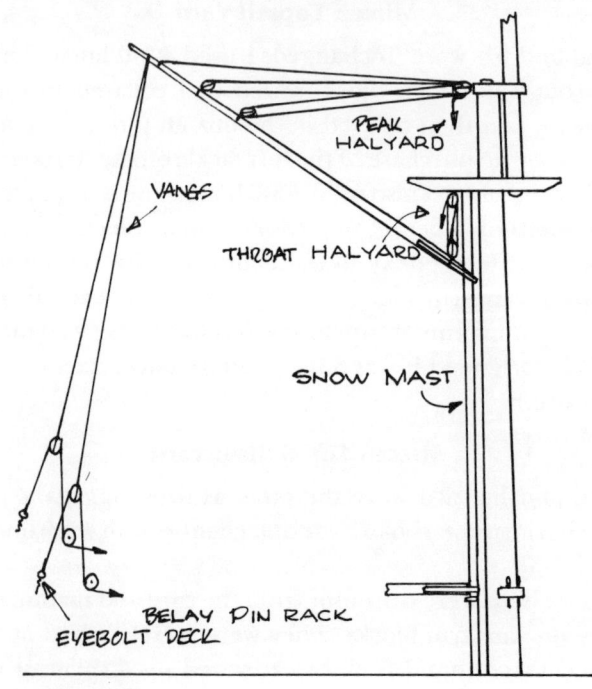

Fig. 114. Spanker gaff

RUNNING RIGGING

mizzenmast cap. Subsequently, it reeved through two, 1/8-in. single blocks, was seized along the gaff with a final reeving through the triple block to fall and be belayed on the mizzenmast pin rack. (The original was 3 in. circumference.)

Vangs. I used #2-0 linen. These were secured with a clove hitch to the aft gaff. The pendant was seized to a becket, stropped to a 1/8-in. single block, with the standing end secured to eyebolt in deck near aft mizzen rail. It was then reeved through a single block, stropped in a deck eyebolt and finally brought through the bulwark sheave to be belayed on aft bulwark pin rack, as shown in Fig. 114. (The original was 3 in. circumference.)

Flag Halyard. I used #3-0 linen. The flag halyard was reeved through a small, 1/16-in. block, stropped to an eyebolt in the end of the gaff, and belayed to small cleats in the aft inboard transom area.

Throat Halyard. I used #2-0 linen. A single 1/8-in. block was seized and collared around a proximal gaff and through the sides of the jaws. A 1/8-in. double block was stropped to an eyebolt secured into the middle of the aft mizzenmast head between the crosstrees. The standing end of the halyard was seized to a becket in the single block then reeved through the double block, the single block, and again the double block successively with the fall belaying on the mizzen pin rack. (The original was 3 in. circumference.)

Spanker Boom

Topping Lift. I used #2-0 linen. See Fig. 115. The topping lift was begun clove hitched to the aft segment of the boom, then run upwards to be reeved through 1/8-in. single blocks (boxwood or cherry), stropped and eyebolted to both aft outboard trestletrees and then brought down to be seized to an 1/8-in. double block, connected by a fall to a 1/8-in. single block, stropped and eyebolted into the deck. The fall was belayed to the side pin rack. (The original was 3 in. circumference.)

Guy Pendant. I used #2-0 linen. The aft of the boom near the transom rail was seized and spliced with a 1/8-in. double block. A 1/8-in. single block was stropped on an iron traveler which was attached to the spar deck traveler bar, close to the transom rail. The standing end was seized on a becket on the single block, then reeved through the double block with the fall cleated to a port or starboard cleat depending on the sailing tack at the time (starboard model).

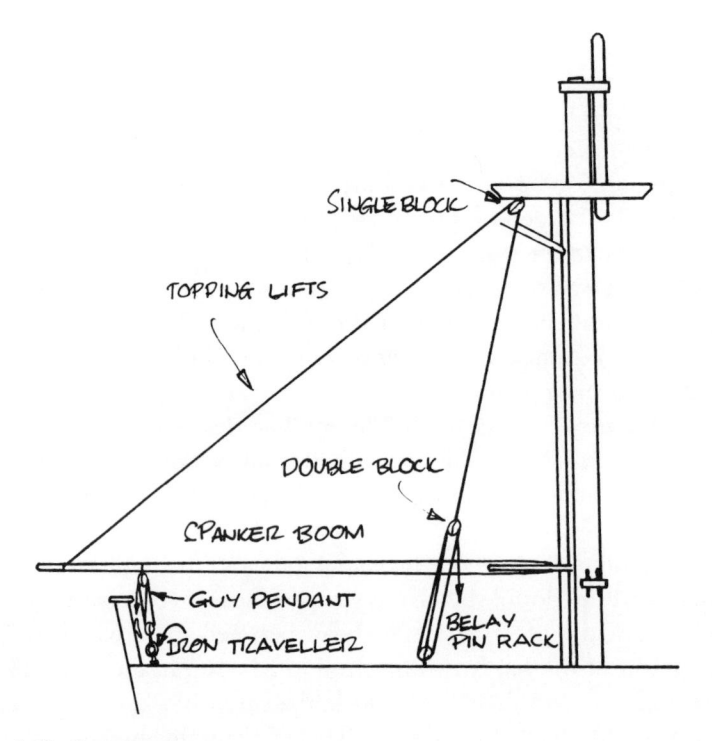

Fig. 115. Spanker boom

Spritsail

The use of the spritsail was largely abandoned in the early nineteenth century but has been included on model as shown in Fig. 116.

Truss. A small 1/16-in. ribbed parral could be used, or the standard truss method could be employed with luff tackle eyebolted to the bow bulwark and the fall belayed to the bowsprit bow timbers or knightheads. Included in the drawing (Fig. 116) are the jibboom and flying jibboom shrouds (4 in., 3-1/2 in., and 2-3/4 in., respectively), which on the model were constructed of #1 black silk, each one seized on its respective boom and then seized on bull's-eyes with appropriate #3-0 silk lanyard stropped to 1/8-in. bull's-eyes, secured to eyebolts on the fore side of the catheads as illustrated.

Lifts. See Fig. 117. I used #2-0 linen. Lifts were begun seized on eyebolts in the mast bowsprit cap, reeved through 1/8-in. cherry blocks seized to the yardarm ropes, reeved back through 1/8-in. blocks stropped to eyebolt in the lower part of the bowsprit cap to fall and be

RUNNING RIGGING   135

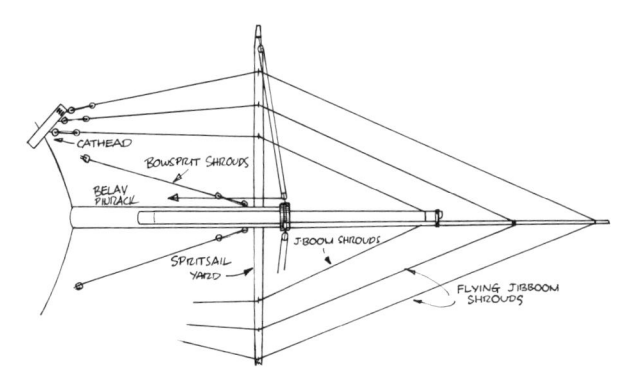

Fig. 116. Jibboom and flying jibboom shrouds

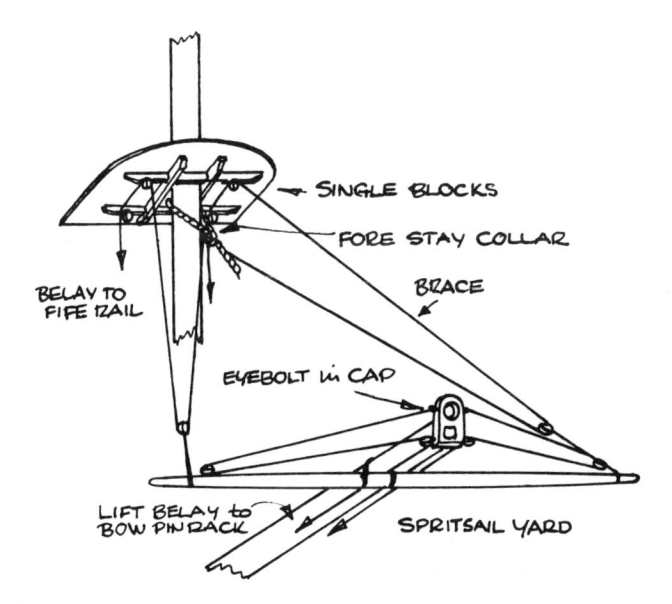

Fig. 117. Spritsail yard

belayed on the bow pin rack as shown in Fig. 117. (The original was 3 in. circumference.)

Braces. I used #2-0 linen. The braces were begun seized to a collar at the forestay sling, reeved through a 1/8-in. brace block, and then subsequently through two successive 1/8-in. blocks, stropped to eyebolts in the fore and aft sections of the crosstrees of the foremast top to fall and be belayed to the port and starboard pin racks (Fig. 117). (The original was 3 in. circumference.)

Sails

With the exception of the quarter and clew garnet blocks, lashed to the lower yards, the lines for the sails and attending rigging were not included in this book as they were not incorporated on the model. The number of lines required for each sail would unnecessarily clutter the model in my opinion. For historical interest, a diagram of a standard sail arrangement is included in Fig. 118. It is also included for those who might wish to (God love 'em) make a large scale model of the *Constellation* complete with sails and attendant rigging.

Stern Boat

The stern boat is as noted in Fig. 119. This plan is of a 28-ft whaleboat similar to that employed on the *Constitution*. This whaleboat is included on the model of the *Constellation* in the World Trade Center in Baltimore. The boat is suspended from the stern davits with two double block tackles, the falls of which are belayed to stern inner bulwark port and starboard cleats near or above the guy pendant cleats. The whaleboat may be included if the modeller chooses. It may be constructed of wood frames of either apple wood or other hardwood and planked with apple wood, basswood, etc. The whaleboat on the model was carved of a solid piece of maple with the thwarts, inner frames, masts, etc., added after the hull was carved and hollowed out. The keel and rudder were made of basswood and added to the curved hull. The

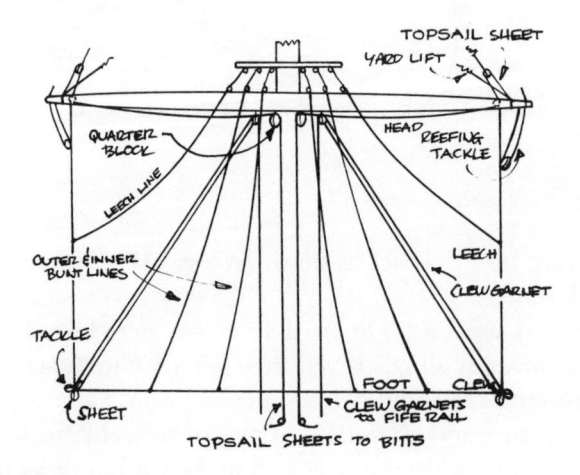

Fig. 118. Sail rigging

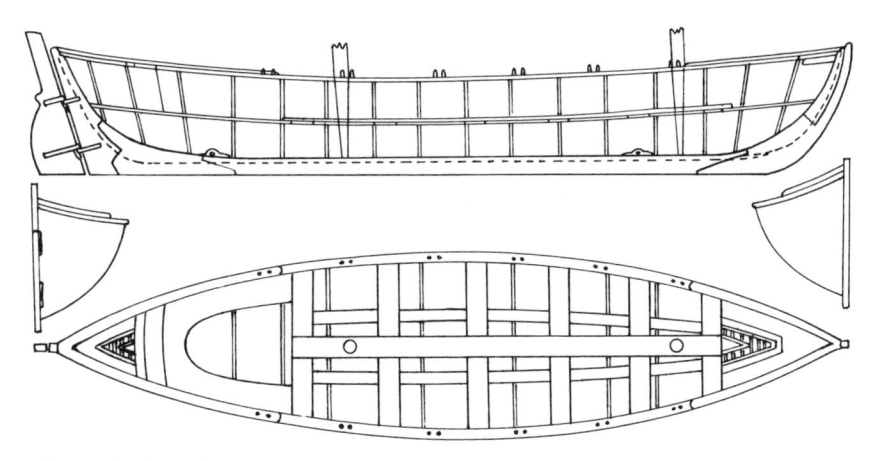

Fig. 119. Stern boat

inboard area was varnished. The outside planking was painted flat white with a black upper gunwale stripe. It should be mentioned that the simulated planking corresponded with carvel planking although there may have been some clinker built whaleboats made during the *Constellation* era. In all probability, on the original *Constellation*, there were several aft port and starboard davits for cutters or whaleboats similar to the *President* and *Constitution*. Also, there may have been some whaleboats stacked midships on temporary beams over the ship's gun deck. This remains conjectural, however, as there is no extant historical evidence for proof. Prevention of damage to these small boats was obviously impossible during combat. It may also suggest that the open bulwarks at the spar deck level as noted on the Doughty draught and present on the model of the *Constellation* in the Smithsonian probably never existed. Commodore Truxton would have undoubtedly preferred to have six or eight inches of oak planking between himself and the sea or foe similar to the other frigates authorized for construction by the Congress in the 1790s.

(A) The completed model

(B) Bow detail

(C) Stern detail

(D) Midship detail

Bibliography

Although not all of the following deal specifically with the *Constellation*, they will be useful to modellers of period ships.

Anderson, Romola and Anderson, R. C. *The Sailing Ship*. New York: Bonanza, 1963.

Bowen, John. *Scale Model Sailing Ships*. London: Conway Maritime Press Ltd., 1978.

Chapelle, Howard I. and Polland, Leon. *The Constellation Question*. Washington, D.C.: Smithsonian Institution Press, 1970.

Davis, Charles G. *The Built-Up Ship Model*. Salem: Marine Research Society, 1933.

Ship Model Builder's Assistant. Salem: Marine Research Society, 1926.

Edson, Merritt, ed. *Ship Modeler's Shop Notes*. Washington, D.C.: Nautical Research Guild, Inc., 1979.

Grimwood, V. R. *American Ship Models*. New York: W. W. Norton & Co., 1952.

Johnson, Gene. *Ship Model Building*. Centreville, Md.: Cornell Maritime Press, 1961.

Longridge, C. Nepean. *The Anatomy of Nelson's Ships*. Hemel Hempstead, Herts., England: Model and Allied Publications, Ltd., 1955.

McNarry, Donald. *Ship Models in Miniature*. New York: Praeger Publishers, 1975.

Parker, George S. *Five Historic Ships from Plan to Model*. Centreville, Md: Cornell Maritime Press, 1979.

Polland, Leon. Communications with the author, 1977. "The Frigate *Constellation*: An Outline of Present Restoration." *Society of Naval Architects and Marine Engineers* (1966): 1-131.

Randolph, Evan. "USS *Constellation*, 1797 to 1979." *The American Neptune* (October 1979): 235.

Scarlett, Charles, Polland, Leon, et al. "Yankee Race Horse: The USS *Constellation*," *Maryland Historical Magazine*, 56 (March 1961): 15-31.

Steel, David. *Steel's Elements of Mastmaking, Sail Making and Rigging*. Edited by Claude Gill. New York: Sweetman, 1932.

Underhill, Harold A. *Plank on Frame Models*. 2 vols. Glasgow: Brown, Son and Ferguson, Ltd., 1976.

Williams, Guy R. *The World of Model Ships and Boats*. New York: G. P. Putnam's Sons, 1971.

Wingrove, Gerald A. *The Techniques of Ship Modelling*. Watford, Herts., England: Model and Allied Publications, 1976.

Index

Ammunition scuttles, 54
Anchor, 76-77
    bitts, 56
    pads, 70
    pawls, 66, 67
    releasing device, 77

Backstays, 116
Baseboard, 4, 5
Beams, deck, 22-24
Bearding line, 18
Becket, 109
Belaying pins, 105-7
Belfry, 80
Bilge pumps, 54
Binnacle, 79-80
Bitts, anchor, 56
    bowsprit, 66-67
    deck, 63-65
Blocks. *See* Rigging
Boat, stern, 136-37
Boom, gaff, 102
    spanker, 102
Bowsprit, 98-100
    dimensions, 105
    dolphin striker, 100
    flying jibboom, 99
    gammoning hole, 76
    jibboom, 99
    pin rack, 70-71

Braces, 127. *See also* individual yards
Breast hooks, 27
Bumpkin, main brace, 49-50
Buttock lines, 10

Camber, 21
Cannonade, 81-83
Cannonball racks, 54
Cannons, 59-60
Capstan, 53
Captain's castles, 46-48
    furniture, 51-53
Carriages, gun, 57-59
Catharpins, 115-16
Cathead, 68-69
Cat's face, 68
Chain plates, 88-90
Channels, 86-87
Cheeks, mast, 93
Crosstrees, dimensions, 96-97, 103

Davits, 49-50
Deadeyes, chain plates, 88-90
    construction, 87-88
    lanyard, 111
Deadwood, 68-69
Deck, spar, 23, 61, 78
Deck beams, 22-24
Decks, 20-22
Dolphin striker, 100

Ekeings, 76
Eyebolt key, 105-7

False keel, 9
Fife rails, 66
Fish plates, 67
Flemish horse, 125
Fore royal yard, 129
    topgallant yard, 128
    topsail yard, 127
    yard, 126
Frame, bolts, 23
    cant, 11-14
    fairing, 13
    futtocks, 10-11
    jig, 5
    timberheads, 37
Frames, 9-14

Galley, 55-56
Gammoning, bowsprit, 121-22
Gangway, spar deck, 60-63
Garboard strake, 31
Gudgeons, 33
Gun carriages, 57-60
    lids, 40-43
    ports, 34, 37-38
    sills, 35
    tackles, 60-61
Guy pendant, 133

Half breadth lines, 10
Halyard, flag, 133
    peak, 132
    throat, 133
Halyards. *See* individual yards
Hatch, construction, 25-26

Hatch ladders, 45
Hawseholes, 73
Head knees, 74-76
Head rails, 74-76
Hearteyes, 118
Hogging, 9
Horse, 125. *See also* individual yards

Jackstays, 125
Jacob's ladder, 118
Jig, deck lines, 21, 22
    frame, 5
    plank, 33-34

Keel, 5, 9, 12
Keelson, 18
Kennel frame, 69
Knees, daggar, 23
    hanging, 24
    lodge, 24
Knighthead, 68
Knot, Matthew Walker, 110

Ladders, gangway, 61
    hatch, 45
Lashing, 109
Lift, topping, spanker boom, 133
Lifts. *See* individual yards
Lofting, 9, 10
Lubber's hole, 94

Main mast, 90
    royal yard, 131
    topgallant yard, 131
    topsail yard, 130
    yard, 129

INDEX

Mast bands, 96
   bibbs, 93
   bolsters, 93, 96
   caps, 95-96
   cheeks, 93
   coats, 98
   crosstrees, 104
   dimensions, 92, 103
   fid plates, 94, 97
   rubbing paunch, 91
   snow, 100
   steps, 18, 36-37
   tops, 93, 94, 103-4
Mizzen royal yard, 120
   topgallant yard, 131
   topsail yard, 131
   yard, 131

Nelson's stripe, 43

Orlop deck, 20

Painting, general, 38-40
   Nelson's stripe, 43
   quarter galleries, 48
Parcelling, 110
Parrals, 102. *See also* individual yards
Partition, 51-53
Pendant, masthead, 115-16
Pin racks, 105-6
Pintles, 33
Planking, 29-34
Planks, fastening, 29-30
Plank-sheer, 14, 31, 68, 78
Plank "stealers," 31

Quarter galleries, 17, 46-48

Quoin, carriage, 59

Rabbet lines, 7, 8, 18
Railings, spar deck, 62-63
Rake, mast, 37
Ratlines, 112-15
Rigging, running, 125-35
   standing, 108-24
Rope, types, 109-10
Rudder, 17, 33

Sails, 136
Scarfs, types, 9
Scuppers, 29
Seat rails, 74-76
Seizing, 109
Serving, 110
Shot pots, 21, 54
Shrouds, Bentinck, 115
   bowsprit, 122
   general construction, 110-12
   topgallant mast, 116-17
   topmast, 116-17
Skylights, 78-79
Sling, foreyard, 125
   mainyard, 129
   mizzen (crossjack) yard, 131
Snaking, 119
Spalls, 14
Spar deck. *See* Deck, spar
Spars, general length rule, 92
Spritsail braces, 135
   dimensions, 105
   lifts, 134-35
   truss, 134
   yard, 134-35

Stanchions, fife rails, 64-66
    mast top rails, 95
    orlop deck, 27
    spar deck, 62
Starburst, stern, 48-49
Stays, back, 116
    bob, 122
    flying jib, 124
    fore and fore preventer, 118-19
    fore royal, 124
    fore topgallant, 122
    fore topmast, 122
    fore topmast preventer, 122
    jib, 122
    main and main preventer, 117-18
    main topgallant, 121
    main-topmast, 120
    main-topmast preventer, 120
    martingales, 124
    mizzen, 119-20
    mizzen royal, 120
    mizzen topmast, 120
Steering wheel, 83-85
Stem, billet head, 71
    scroll, 71
Stempieces, 6, 7, 8, 71-73
Steps, mast, 36-37
Stern, detail, 48-50
Stern boat, 136-37
Stern post, 6-8
Sternson, 8
Strongback, 5
Strop, 109
Surgical tie, 113

Swallow, block, 111
"Swifter," 112

Teredos, 6
Tiller, 33, 85,
Timberheads, 66-68
Topgallant mast, 96, 97
Topmast, 96, 97
Trail cheeks, 71-73
Transom, counter timbers, 15-17
    eagle, 49
    molding, 49
    planking, 31-32
    seats, 17, 50-51
    starburst, 48-49
    transverse timbers, 17
Trunnels, 7, 11, 34
Truss. *See* individual yards

Vangs, 133

Wale, ceiling, 34
Waterlines, 10
Waterways, 27-28
    spar deck, 61
Whaleboat, 136-37
Windows, stern, 39
Worming, 109

Yards, battens, 101
    dimensions, 105
    general construction, 100-2
    jackstays, 100-1
    stirrups, 100-1